C000285562

A guide to the Pennine Way

SCOTLAND

Berwick upon Tweed

Route of the Pennine Way ———

Land over 800 ft ▓

0   5   20
miles

BORDERS

• Hawick

Cheviot Hills

NORTHUMBERLAND

North Tyne

Roman Wall

Carlisle •

South Tyne

Tyne

Newcastle upon Tyne •

Eden

• Penrith

Vale of Eden

P
E
N
N
I
N
E
S

Teesdale

• Durham

DURHAM

• Darlington

Tees

CUMBRIA

Kendal •

Swaledale

Wensleydale

Ure

Swale

• Ripon

Lancaster •

Airedale

• Harrogate

YORKSHIRE

LANCASHIRE

Burnley •

• Blackburn

Aire

• Leeds

Bradford •

Calder

• Huddersfield

Bolton •

Manchester •

CHESHIRE

The Peak

Buxton •

• Sheffield

DERBYSHIRE

A guide to
the Pennine Way

Christopher John Wright

Constable London

First published in Great Britain 1967
by Constable and Company Ltd
3 The Lanchesters, 162 Fulham Palace Road
London W6 9ER
Copyright © 1967 Christopher John Wright
Reprinted 1968
2nd edition 1975
3rd edition 1979
Reprinted 1981
4th edition 1987
5th edition 1991
Reprinted 1996
ISBN 0 09 470640 9
Printed in Great Britain by
BAS Printers Ltd, Over Wallop, Hampshire

By the same author and published by Constable:
A Guide to the Pilgrims' Way & North Downs Way
A Guide to Offa's Dyke Path
A Guide to the Pembrokeshire Coast Path

Published by Cicerone Press:
The Westmorland Heritage Walk

Contents

Among the projects designed to extend walking facilities in the National Parks was the promotion of the first long-distance route called the Pennine Way, which runs northwards from the Peak in Derbyshire along the moorland spine of northern England as far as the Scottish Border, a total distance of 250 miles/402 km.

The idea of this continuous footpath was first suggested by the late Tom Stephenson, journalist and rambler, and was largely inspired by the affinity to the Pilgrims' Way and by the Appalachian Trail and the famous John Muir Trail in the USA. It was on 22 June 1935 that the Daily Herald published Tom Stephenson's now famous article suggesting the creation of a 'long, green trail' along the Pennine chain.

The project quickly gained support, especially among the ramblers' and other open-air organisations, and at a conference held in 1938 representatives unanimously agreed that a Pennine Way was desirable, and that 'the wide, health-giving moorlands and high places of solitude, the features of natural beauty and the places of historical interest along the Pennine Way give this route a special character and attractiveness which should be available for all time as a natural heritage of the youth of the country, and of all who feel the call of the hills and lonely places.' This footpath, it was emphasised, should be nothing more than a way trodden by walkers. Any artificially surfaced track would be as objectionable as a metalled road.

Before the War, members of the Ramblers' Association and the Youth Hostels Association had surveyed the 250 miles/402 km of the proposed route. The results of this survey, which revealed that 90 miles/145 km of new footpaths were needed, were supplied to the National Parks Commission (now renamed the Countryside Commission), who have the responsibility for preparing and submitting to the Secretary of State, Department of the Environment, proposals for the establishment of long-distance routes.

In due course provision was made by the Commission for the development of the Pennine Way as the first of the long-distance paths which may be established under the National Parks and Access to the Countryside Act, 1949, and, after consulting the local authorities concerned, they submitted a report to the Minister for his approval in June, 1951.

On 16 July 1951 official approval for the Pennine Way was granted by Mr Hugh Dalton. The Minister's sanction having been given, the highway authorities were required by the Act to open up the new paths which were needed to complete the route.

On 24 April 1965 the Right Hon. F.T. Willey, MP, Minister of Land and Natural Resources, officially opened the Pennine Way on the moor at Malham. The National Parks Commission was responsible for the event and its chairman, Lord Strang, GCB, GCMG, MBE, and Tom Stephenson for the Ramblers' Association were the speakers. The 200 invited guests—representatives of all the bodies who had put so much work into bringing the scheme into fruition, including the author who was one of the YHA's representatives—were supported by a 2,000 strong band of walkers who could not be included in the list of formal invitations.

Malham Moor was also the venue on 22 June 1985 for a celebration by the Pennine Way Council for the fiftieth anniversary of the idea of the Pennine Way. Hundreds of ramblers gathered at the open air rally. Tom Stephenson, still going strong at ninety-two, was the principal speaker. He died on 1 March 1987, two weeks after his ninety-fourth birthday.

Accommodation
There is now a wide choice of overnight accommodation and refreshment at suitable intervals along the Pennine Way route. Youth hostels, bunkhouses, bed-and-breakfast lodgings and farmhouse accommodation are now widely available.

There is a chain of eighteen youth hostels on or near the Pennine Way, and youth hostellers will find the Pennine Way Bureau invaluable for providing a centralised booking service for youth hostels along the route. A service information pack is free if you send a 6″ × 9″ s.a.e. to Yorkshire Region YHA, 96 Main Street, Bingley, BD16 2JH.

Their accompanying booklet contains useful information about shops and services in the villages along the Way.

For details of accommodation on the Pennine Way route consult the YHA Handbook, the Ramblers' Association Bed and Breakfast Guide, the Cyclists' Touring Club Handbook and the Camping Club of Great Britain Sites List, all of which are reliable in every way. The Pennine Way Council, a consortium of local authorities and organisations having an interest in promoting and protecting the Pennine Way, have published an accommodation list. It cannot claim to be comprehensive, but it is published regularly and includes a camp-sites guide. It can be obtained from information centres and youth hostels along the route, or from the Secretary, The Pennine Way Council, 89 Radford Road, Lewisham, London, SE13 6SB.

From 10 June to 10 September Trans Pennine Transport operates a direct door-to-door minibus service linking Edale and Kirk Yetholm with Manchester, Sheffield, Leeds and Newcastle. In addition, they run a sherpa service carrying rucksacks and passengers along the route of the Pennine Way. They can transport your rucksack for you and have it at your destination when you arrive. Similarly, if you want to miss out some stages, owing to fatigue, illness or weather, then TPT Sherpa will take you on to your next stop. For information, write to Trans Pennine Transport, 3/25 Cathcart Hill, London N19 5QN, or phone 0756 753146.

Route finding

The Pennine Way provides some of the roughest walking to be found in Britain, but in good weather it is within the capacity of anyone able to undertake 12–15 miles/19–24 km of hill-walking a day, sometimes across boggy ground or through expanses of heather and moor grass. In rain, mist, snow or high winds it can prove arduous and even exhausting for the hardiest walkers, and should certainly not be attempted in such conditions by anyone unable to steer a course by map and compass.

Tens of thousands of walkers have now 'done' the Pennine Way. Their feet have worn deep grooves in it and occasionally in the patience of farmers whose land it crosses. It varies from the Indianfile track crossing pastures (where it is least defined) to an extended quagmire several feet wide on the peaty moorland. It has been reinforced in places with stretches of plastic carpet and steps up steep slopes. So severe is the erosion on the southern half of the Pennine Way that the Countryside Commission, the Peak Park Planning Board and the Yorkshire Dales National Park are embarking on ambitious three-year projects of erosion control and management of the Pennine Way between Edale and Littleborough and the three Peaks area, and have appointed Pennine Way Management Project Officers to organise volunteer and Community Programme teams of conservation workers.

The Countryside Commission have erected some two dozen notice boards—about 8ft/2.4 m high and 3 ft/0.9 m wide—at various points throughout the route, showing local sections of 1:25,000 scale maps, laminated in plastic, giving brief advice about equipment and the Country Code. They have deteriorated very badly over the years and have never been much use to the Pennine Wayfarer: you can't take the maps with you and the route between the notice boards is too complex to memorise. These maps are situated at the following places:

1 Edale—at the start of the Pennine Way.
2 Crowden—outside the Pennine Way hostel.
3 Standedge—opposite the Floating Light PH.
4 Blackstone Edge—on A58 at The White House PH.
5 Ponden—on road at W end of reservoir.
6 Lothersdale—at farm next to Hare & Hounds PH.
7 Gargrave—on car park beside bridge over R. Aire.
8 Malham—beside public toilets next to Buck Inn.
9 Horton in Ribblesdale—on car park near public toilets near The Crown PH.
10 Hawes—in main street, near car park and public toilets.
11 Thwaite—in village street, next to telephone call box.
12 Bowes—at A66/A67 road junction
13 Middleton in Teesdale—in main street, next to public toilets.
14 Teesdale—at Widdybank Farm.
15 Dufton—on village green.

16 Garrigill—by church gates, near George & Dragon PH.

17 Slaggyford—in centre of village.

18 Greenhead—in lay-by on A69 E of Gap Shields.

19 Hadrians Wall—at Steel Rigg car park and public toilets N of Once Brewed.

20 Bellingham—in village street on car park next to public toilets.

21 Lords Shaw—at cattle grid on road N of Lords Shaw.

22 Byrness—on The Raw picnic site.

23 Windy Gyle.

24 Kirk Yetholm—on village green.

The Pennine Way walker will require a compass and the following 1:50,000 scale Landranger (Second Series) maps:

74 Kelso

80 The Cheviot Hills

86 Haltwhistle & Bewcastle

91 Appleby

92 Barnard Castle & Richmond

98 Wensleydale & Wharfedale

103 Blackburn & Burnley

109 Manchester

110 Sheffield & Huddersfield

The following 1:25,000 scale Outdoor Leisure maps will also be useful:

The Dark Peak

South Pennines

Malham & Upper Wharfedale

The Three Peaks

The maps in this book are at a scale of approximately one half inch to one mile. The official route, and the official alternatives for bad weather, are marked by a broken line.

When the author first walked the Pennine Way, whilst still a teenager, in 1962, the only 'guide' available was a 6d leaflet from the Ramblers' Association giving route directions, compass bearings and grid references to enable the walker to plot the route of the Pennine Way on his Ordnance Survey maps. Since this book first appeared in August 1967 there have been many other Pennine Way 'guidebooks' published. Whilst only one or two can be called true walkers' guides, a complete list is given in the bibliography on p. 229, and readers will be able to compare the relative merits of each.

1 Be properly clad
Wear strong boots and adequate windproof clothing. Carry spare woollens and a waterproof. Even in summer it can be cold on a mountain top.

2 Carry essential equipment
Always carry a compass and a 1:50,000 map, or better, a 1:25,000 map of the district, and be certain that with their aid you can steer a safe course in mist or darkness. Carry also a whistle and an electric torch (with spare bulb and battery). Carry energy giving food—such as chocolate, glucose and dried fruits.

3 Allow yourself ample time
The moors and fells are vast and should be treated with respect. Winter days are short, and even in summer bad weather may delay your progress. Add to a normal walking time of one hour for 3 miles/4.8 km, one hour for each 1,500 ft/457 m of ascent. Following the Pennine Way from Edale to Kirk Yetholm involves climbing approximately 32,000 ft/9 754m in addition to 250 miles/402 km measured from the map. In a publicity leaflet the Countryside Commission states: 'Bearing in mind that the frequent changes in direction and level of the path make straight line map reading unrealistic, an allowance of about 25% should be added to get a truer idea of the distances involved.'

4 Say where you are going
Before you set out in the morning, leave word of your intended route and destination. Search parties like to know at least in which direction to start.

5 Watch the weather
Clouds often form quickly on mountain tops, so be sure of your bearing before landmarks are hidden in mist. Weather conditions

can change rapidly. Do not hesitate to turn back. Know the local weather forecast.

6   Safety in numbers
Think twice before going on the hills alone. There should be at least three in a party, for if an accident occurs one can stay with the patient while the third seeks help.

7   Distress signal
In an emergency, give the recognised distress signal of six blasts on a whistle or six flashes of a torch in one minute, followed by a minute's silence, repeated as necessary. The answering signal is three blasts or flashes in a minute, followed by a minute's silence and then repeated.

The Countryside Commission have prepared the Country Code as a guide to visitors, some of whom are perhaps unaccustomed to country ways. Please remember and observe the following standards of good manners when you go to enjoy the beauties and the pleasures of the garden that is Britain's countryside.

1   Guard against all risks of fire
Don't drop lighted matches or cigarette ends, particularly near crops, plantations, woods, heaths and hay ricks. A fire, once started, is difficult to put out.

2   Fasten all gates
Fasten all gates, unless they are obviously intended to be left open. Animals can do great damage to crops and to themselves if they stray. They may be injured by traffic or be the cause of accidents.

3   Keep dogs under proper control
Animals are easily frightened by strange dogs, so do not let them disturb cattle, hens or sheep; keep your dog on its lead when near other animals or walking along the road.

4   Keep to paths across farm land
Avoid damaging crops in any way. Corn, grass and hay that have been trampled flat are difficult to harvest. Do not trespass.

5   Avoid damaging fences, hedges and walls
Where a man can go, an animal will follow, and damage to crops will result. Use gates and stiles where they are provided.

6   Do not leave litter
Take your litter home, including bottles and tins. All litter is not only unsightly but dangerous. Broken glass, opened tins and plastic bags can very easily harm livestock and damage farm machinery.

7   Safeguard water supplies
A stream, brook or well may be the only water supply for a farmer
and his animals. Water is precious in the country. Do not pollute it
in any way.

8   Protect wild life, plants and trees
Never dig up plants and flowers, carve on trees, and please do not
take birds' eggs. Wild flowers, birds and trees give more pleasure to
more people if left alone.

9   Go carefully on country roads
Blind corners, hump-back bridges, slow-moving farm vehicles and
herds of cattle are all hazards for the motorist, cyclist and walker.
Careless car parking may block the entrance to fields or farmyards.

10   Respect the life of the countryside
Enjoy the countryside, but do not hinder the work of the
countryman. Roads and paths run through the farmer's land, and
animals, machinery and buildings are the raw materials from which
he earns his living. You, the public, are on trust. Be considerate.

The Long Distance Paths Advisory Service (LDPAS) has recently been
set up with support from the Countryside Commission, the Long
Distance Walkers Association and the Ramblers' Association. It has
records of over 400 current and projected long distance routes on file
to help all those interested in planning or using walking routes of
more than 20 miles long in Britain. For further information, please
write to Mr Gerald Cole, Administrator, Long Distance Paths
Advisory Service, The Bar, Holme Lyon, Burneside, Kendal,
Cumbria, LA9 6QX.

Edale to Crowden

Edale
The Pennine Way begins at the top of Edale village, a secluded little place with pretty houses and lovely gardens, but also perhaps the most popular walking centre in the Peak District National Park. The Peak District Warden Service is based in Edale, where there is also a mountain rescue post and a National Park Information Centre with an excellent camp site adjoining. A Youth Hostel is situated some 2 miles/3 km away to the east at Lady Booth Brook. Other accommodation is available at the Rambler Inn (formerly the Church Hotel, but renamed when purchased by Ramblers' Association Services on 14 June 1982), and at Armfield, Upper Booth; while Cooper's Cafe at the head of the village provides refreshments and a camp site.

Kinder Scout
Immediately north of the village is Kinder Scout, an extremely irregular plateau covered with peat bog and extending over 15 sq. miles/39 sq. km. The sides of the plateau are steep and sometimes precipitous, and the streams have cut deep cloughs where sparkling water runs over moss-green boulders, cascading down into innumerable golden pools, with the coarse silver-green moorland grass on either hand. The plateau summit is covered with many large muddy hollows, called 'groughs,' made by the action of water on the spongy soil. Groughs vary in depth from a few feet/metres to 15 ft/4.5 m and more; some are narrow enough to jump and others more than 20 ft/6 m wide. On the map it looks easy, but at all times Kinder presents interesting problems of navigation.

The unusual terrain of the gritstone moor of Kinder Scout reveals rolling contours of bilberry, crowberry and acid-loving grasses. Kinder and Bleaklow receive a mean annual rainfall of 63 inches/160 cm, an ideal climate for the cotton grass sedge, the main plant cover on these high peat moors. The moors are wild and desolate for much of the year but are strikingly transformed by the white mass of cotton grass in June and July and the purple of the heather in September.

The start of the Pennine Way. The log bridge spans Grindsbrook above Edale Village

The moors are the haunt of grouse and curlew, but more widespread is the meadow pipit, a small brown bird which is identified by the white side feathers of the tail as it rises from the ground. Grouse chuckle and cluck among the peat hags and shout 'Goback!' when disturbed. Here you are an immeasurable distance from everywhere, surrounded by sky and black peat.

Main Route over Kinder: 3 miles/5 km
Grindsbrook: the start of the Pennine Way
The southern end of the 250 mile/402 km long Pennine Way is reached by passing northwards through Edale village to the road head and the log bridge over Grindsbrook. A well-defined path leads through the Meadows and a mixed copse to a stile and the crossing of Golden Clough and the wild hollow of Grindsbrook, the most striking of all watercourses on Kinder Scout. As we climb by the wide brown track we can study the geology of Kinder as the valley sides close in.

The plateau of Kinder is formed by a slab of millstone grit, several hundred feet/metres thick, resting on a pedestal of shale. The well-drained shale slopes are littered with landslips and transported rock debris, with heather, bracken and bilberry occurring on the fertile soil. The gritstone is rich in potash and iron, and the soluble material is readily washed out of the porous rock. The steep rugged gritstone cliffs are black from grime and weathering, but the natural colour of this rough granular stone varies from faint gold to brown.

In a little over 1.5 miles/2.4 km from Edale the main stream turns to the north (right), but we continue up the tributary north-west to Fox Holes and the edge of the summit plateau. Continue in the same direction to join the feeder of Crowden Brook, which we follow slightly west of north towards Crowden Head, 2,070 ft/ 632 m.

The peaty wastes are crossed northwest to join the head streams of the River Kinder, which leads north then west to the Downfall. The river flows between some of the deepest groughs on Kinder and the stream bed is flecked with shining white pebbles in silvery sand. The river widens at Kinder Gates, a dramatic gritstone gateway,

Upper Tor

Grindsbrook

Grindslow Knoll

To Sheffield ▶

To Manchester

Kinder Scout and Edale under snow, from Mam Tor Great Ridge

Grindslow Knoll   Anvil Stone Fox Holes   2062´

Ringing Roger

Grindsbrook from Ringing Roger

The author in the peat 'groughs' on Kinder Scout

and the path is then clear to the Downfall, crossing and recrossing the shallow stream as it meanders.

If the clouds are low when you have reached the top of Grindsbrook, a compass bearing of 290 degrees will bring you out at the head of the Downfall, although it will be difficult to follow a straight course. If the weather is really bad, it will be best to avoid the featureless tops and take the alternative route via Upper Booth and Edale Cross.

Alternative Route over Kinder 4.5 miles/7.24 km
Edale to Downfall via Edale Cross
From the road head at the Nags Head in Edale village take the path that leads westwards through a gateway, and follow a stream bed that emerges in the pastures below Grindslow Knoll. (An alternative way to Grindsbrook diverges here, crossing the hillside diagonally northwards to the Sledge Road and the summit of Grindslow Knoll, and the plateau edge to the head of Grindsbrook.) A well-defined path leads below Broad Lee Bank Tor to the hamlet of Upper Booth and the crossing of Crowden Brook by a tiny one arch bridge.

A good track now follows the course of the River Noe, and in less than 1.5 miles/2.4 km the packhorse bridge below Jacob's Ladder is reached. This is on the route of the old packhorse track which crossed the moors between Edale and Hayfield.

Jacob's Ladder rises opposite, a steep track scarring the almost vertical hillside. It was so named because it was first opened up by one Jacob Marshall, who used to send his laden donkey by the easier winding route while he himself went straight up.

The true path leads to the right and not up the boulder strewn scree directly in front. It is easier to climb the slope by taking the donkey track to the left past the ruins of Edale Head House. In the late 1930s/early '40s this farm was standing intact, though empty, and its walls provide the last shelter before crossing Kinder.

On again to Edale Cross at 1,750 ft/541 m, where on the righthand side of the track stands a rudely shaped and badly mutilated cross. The medieval stone was probably erected by Cistercian monks to mark the packhorse route.

The River Kinder at Kinder Gates

We now leave this track and turn right through the gateway by the cross, and take the peaty slopes up to the triangulation station on Kinderlow, at 2,077 ft/633 m. Now continue northwards by a path along the western edge, crossing Red Brook and joining the main Pennine Way route by the Shelter Stone above Kinder Downfall.

Main Route:
Downfall to Snake Pass 4 miles/6.4 km
Kinder Downfall is a fine sight in wet weather when the River Kinder plunges over the precipice. The Downfall is where a great triangular wedge has been hacked out of the western escarpment, and when the river thunders over in full spate the wind is said to blow the spray so high that it can be seen in Stockport, 10 miles/16 km away. The foreground, as you look down 500 ft/152 m or more, is magnificent, and so is the view on a clear day. On the far hillside is the little Mermaid Pool, with the usual legend of the mermaid visiting the pool on Easter Eve, and the sure immortality awaiting him who sees her bathing.

From the head of the Downfall descend along the northern edge north-westerly to Mill Hill, crossing the head of William Clough, then north-easterly on the watershed over Moss Castle passing Featherbed Top to reach the Snake Road at its highest point, 1,680 ft/512 m.

The Snake Road was built in 1820, just before people began to see that the steam engine would inevitably supersede the horse-drawn coach. A Turnpike Act of 1818 sanctioned the building of this road so that Sheffield and Manchester could be more directly linked. The road and pass are so named because the moors hereabouts have been owned by the Cavendish family for a long period, and the snake features prominently in that family's coat of arms.

Kinder Downfall

Snake Pass to Bleaklow 4 miles/6.4 km

From Snake Pass to Doctor's Gate near Old Woman the land is so worn and saturated that the Pennine Way has been diverted along a 0.25 mile/400 m causeway of plastic webbing laid on rafts of brushwood which squelches at every step.

Doctor's Gate is the paved section of a Roman Road which connected forts at Hope and Glossop. It was the only route across the tops before the turnpike road, and is between three and four feet wide. Doctor's Gate may have some connection with William Senior's plans in Chatsworth, where it is referred to as 'Doctor Talbot's Gate' and Camden used the modern form of 'Doctor's Gate' in 1789.

Continuing forward by occasional boundary stakes we go along Devil's Dike, and round the head of Crooked Clough passing Higher Shelf Stones. Less than 100 yds/91 m to the north-east of Higher Shelf Stones summit a USAF Super Fortress crashed during the Berlin Air Lift in 1948. The torn and twisted remains have long since been removed by souvenir-hunters and national park litter wardens.

But we must press on, for Bleaklow is probably harder going than even Kinder. Pass over Shelf Moss and Wain Stones to Bleaklow Head, 2,060 ft/633 m, 10 miles/16 km from Edale.

Walking across Bleaklow takes you where the great silence of the moors is broken only by the cries of moor-haunting birds—the red grouse, the lovely call of the curlew, the plaintive cries of the lapwing, and the liquid notes of the golden plover.

Public access to the moorland areas of Kinder, Bleaklow, Langsett, Longdendale and Chew will be restricted on some days in the grouse shooting season, 12th August to 10th December. Arrangements have been made with the landowners by the Peak Park Planning Board for shooting to be confined to limited areas on any one day, thus leaving a greater part of the area accessible. Access is not suspended on Sundays and rights of way are not affected. Please consult notice boards and avoid those areas where shooting is due to take place.

Grouse shooting and sheep are part of the scene and part of the economy of the countryside, but in recent years the relative value of sheep grazing as against grouse shooting has materially changed.

Plastic carpet at the Snake Pass

On Sheep

Sheep are of greatest importance, and these hill and moorland areas are used primarily for sheep grazing. The Derbyshire Gritstone breed predominates. It can readily be recognised, having a black and white speckled face and legs, grey fleece and no horns. The Swaledale is smaller than the Gritstone, but has horns, black face and greyish nose. Next in number are the Scotch Blackface—a horned sheep with distinctive black face—and Lonk, which resembles Gritstone in many ways but is slightly larger and has horns. The Whitefaced Woodland, a white-faced, horned sheep, is somewhat rarer.

On the lower ground heavier breeds are kept, such as the Kerry Hill, Cluns and Hampshires. These sheep need better food and kinder weather, and are much more dependent on supplementary feeding than are the hill breeds.

Bleaklow to Longdendale 3 miles/5 km

From Bleaklow Head descend due north to the head of Wildboar Grain then westerly to John Track Well and Torside Clough, and from the confluence of two streams climb on to the mound of Torside Castle. Take a course east and north of the Castle over the top of Clough Edge, and then take the footpath down to Reaps in Longdendale. There were proposals for an additional Trans-Pennine Motorway to the M62 that would run through Longdendale to connect Manchester with Sheffield, but it has been shelved. It had been argued that as the valley had already been scarred by road, rail, electricity and reservoirs a new motorway would have made very little difference. The desirability and need for such a road was questioned, and as the route passed through a National Park the proposal raised much opposition.

Longdendale

A track leads to the Glossop road, route B6105, where you cross over the disused Manchester–Sheffield (Woodhead) railway and take the track over the dam at the foot of Torside Reservoir, and path to route A628, the Sheffield-Manchester trunk road.

From the road take a footpath north to Highstones Farm, where

Hey Edge

Bareholme Moss

Hostel

B6105

Crowden-in-Longdendale

you can refresh yourself at a delicious spring which issues near an old barn, and descend to Crowden Brook and the youth hostel (2 miles/3.2 km from Reaps, 15 miles/24 km from Edale).

The hostel at Crowden was opened on 4 June, 1965, by Mr Willey, Minister of Land and Natural Resources. The hostel has been converted from six cottages, but visitors do not have to be YHA members to stay overnight, or use the cafe which is open daily. The hostel was built on the initiative of the Peak Park Planning Board, with an Exchequer grant, a lease from Manchester Corporation, and the whole is managed by the Youth Hostels Association.

It has been a strenuous day's walk to reach Crowden, the first place of accommodation since leaving Edale. The next stage, although not quite such hard going, involves longer distances if accommodation is sought at a youth hostel. There is a gap in the hostel chain here as the next one—at Mankinholes—is 27 miles/43.5 km away. (The former hostel at Marsden is now closed.) Other suitable lodgings are harder to find, but your next stop could be at the privately owned Globe Farm Bunkhouse at Standedge, 10 miles/16 km from Crowden.

Crowden to Standedge

Longdendale

Longdendale is an important valley carrying communications between Manchester and Sheffield. It lay in Cheshire (now in the GMC; Greater Manchester County), the reason being that the Earls of Chester laid claim to this 'corridor' route to avoid having to pay the toll on salt which would have been claimed had Longdendale belonged to Derbyshire or Lancashire. One of the salt routes from Cheshire's brine pits followed Longdendale into Yorkshire, and it was made a turnpike road in 1731.

In 1848 the Etherow was dammed up to form the present chain of reservoirs to serve Manchester with water. Completed in 1862 they now have a total capacity of 3,000 million gallons/13 638 million litres. The flanks of Longdendale are jealously guarded by the North West Water Authority. The purity of supply is protected by restriction, and soil treatments, ploughing and cattle grazing are prohibited.

Crowden to Black Hill 5 miles/8 km

The Pennine Way after leaving Crowden follows its original line above Laddow Rocks, and not by Hey Edge and Westend Moss as shown on some maps.

Retrace your steps along the lane past the hostel, turning left to the crossing of Crowden Great Brook. Pass through the gate and after a short distance along the track bear north along the line marking the western boundary of a firing range. The footpath rises gradually towards the cliffs on the skyline, and when the edge of the moor is reached bear right and continue along the crest of the outcrop. This is a favourite gritstone outcrop for the rock climber, and a cave at the base of the cliffs provides shelter in bad weather.

From Laddow Rocks continue in a northerly direction contouring round above Crowden Great Brook, then bear north-easterly over Dun Hill to its source on Black Hill, 1,908 ft/582 m. Here Holme Moss BBC radio and television transmitter comes into view to the south-east. The 750 ft/228 m mast was built in 1950 and it is visible from a great distance. Brilliant flashing white lights on the mast highlight its visibility.

To reach Black Hill we have had to cross Soldier's Lump, a vast peat moss, windswept and lifeless. The name is derived from the bench mark used by the men of the Ordnance Survey when they were mapping the area in 1936, although local tradition has it that soldiers were stationed there during the Luddite Riots of 1811–16 (which seems most improbable). The soldiers had unpleasant memories of their work on the 'prodigious muck heap', for the peaty ground would not hold their tent pegs, and several times their only shelter was whirled away into the mists.

Away to the east is the road to Huddersfield, where once stood a famous old coaching inn called 'Bill' o' Jacks'. Here in 1832, William Bradbury, commonly known as Bill o' Jacks, aged 85 years, and his son Thomas, were found one morning dead on the parlour floor. Suspicion alighted on two poachers, also named Bradbury, who were open enemies of the murdered men. William and Thomas Bradbury were gamekeepers as well as innkeepers, and were due to give evidence against the poachers at Pontefract Assizes. The mystery was never solved, the two poachers being acquitted by an English court of law, which should remove all doubt.

Alternative Route:
Black Hill to Standedge 6.5 miles/10.45 km
Black Hill and White Moss are not for the faint-hearted, and in bad weather it is advisable to descend north-east from Black Hill down the head of Hey Clough. After a while a boundary ditch is reached on the left, and this is followed in a straight line to the road A635 a few yards/metres west of the demolished Isle of Skye Inn.

The famous Isle of Skye Inn stood on Wessenden Head near the Meltham road junction, and has saved the life of more than one benighted rambler. Like the equally famous Bill o' Jacks it has been pulled down, under pretence of still 'purer' water. Some of us would have preferred to take our chances with the water as it was and preserve the inns, but the reservoir-makers would not hear of it. One after another these old inns, which had done good service for scores of years, have been pulled down on the grounds of 'pollution' and now it is hard to find an inn anywhere near a catchment area.

Chesterton's 'Noah' didn't care where the water went so long as it didn't get into the wine, but the Manchester Corporation didn't care where the beer went so long as it didn't get into the water!

This alternative route crosses the road by the site of the Isle of Skye Inn and strikes north-east to a track from the Meltham road. This track is followed down the Wessenden valley and its series of reservoirs, but 0.3 mile/0.48 km below Wessenden Reservoir it crosses the stream by a footbridge. The route follows the stream westerly round the north side of Black Moss and joins the main route at the south-east corner of the farthest reservoir.

Main Route:
Black Hill to Standedge 5 miles/8 km
From Black Hill the Pennine Way route continues north-west over Wessenden Head Moor via height 1,622 ft/507 m to the road crossing near the 20th milestone on the Greenfield-Holmfirth road A635. A mobile tea hut usually occupies the layby at the West Yorkshire—Greater Manchester County boundary. It was near here that the bodies of murdered children were discovered early in 1966, whose executors were brought to justice in the Moors Murders Trial. Myra Hindley and Ian Brady were given sentences of life imprisonment for the murder of Lesley Ann Downey, aged ten, who was found on Hollin Brow Knoll, while 300m away on the other side of the road was the grave of John Kilbride, also aged ten. On Tuesday 16 December 1986 Hindley was flown by police helicopter from prison in Kent to Saddleworth Moor to assist police in finding the graves of Keith Bennett, twelve, and Pauline Reade, sixteen, whose bodies had remained undiscovered for twenty-two years.

Another causeway of brushwood, old pallets and palings strikes north from the A635 for $\frac{1}{4}$ ml/400 m across White Moss and Black Moss, keeping roughly on the watershed between the Saddleworth and Wessenden valleys along a boundary line marked in places by piles of peat. (The boundary is too far west on 1:50,000 maps, but is correct on 1:25,000 maps.) The route runs along the bank of the westernmost reservoir to a packhorse road north of Round Hill, and this is followed to route A62 in Standedge Cutting, 8 miles/12.8 km from Black Hill, 23 miles/36.8 km from Edale.

Standedge Cutting

A mobile tea hut usually occupies a lay-by at the W end of the cutting, and other refreshments may be obtained during licensing hours at the Floating Light public house to the W of the cutting (the nearest) or at the Great Western public house at the E end of the cutting. Overnight accommodation is harder to find, but bunkhouse or B & B may be possible at Globe Farm, some ¾ml/1320m W down the main road A62 towards Saddleworth.

Below Standedge to the west is Cattleshaw Roman Fort, built by Agricola about AD 80. There are two camps, one inside the other. The inner one, about ⅝ of an acre/3 618 sq. metres, is a rectangle, one of the sides abutting the larger camp, which covers about 3 acres/1.2 ha. The ramparts are chiefly piled sods, with a ditch round the outside. The rampart is still 18 ft/5.5 m thick in places, and is doubled from the north to the south-west corner. At each corner once stood a raised platform or tower. The fort seems to have been abandoned about AD 125, in the reign of Hadrian, when its garrison may have been sent north to work on the great Roman Wall.

Standedge to Blackstone Edge

Standedge to Windy Hill 4 miles/6.4 km

Standedge presents a formidable obstacle to transport: roads go
over these hills and railways and canals go underneath them. A
double tunnel under Standedge carries the Huddersfield Narrow
Canal between Marsden and Diggle under one arch, and the railway
through the other. This is the highest canal tunnel in Britain—638
ft/194 m altitude—and also the longest—5,415 yds/4951 m. There
are connections between the canal tunnel and the railway tunnel by
sloping galleries. There is no towpath: boats were worked through it
by 'legging'. The canal is now closed to traffic.

At Standedge we leave the Peak District National Park. From the
A635 to the A62 at Standedge and through to A640 the Pennine
Way largely follows the boundary between Greater Manchester and
West Yorkshire. A rough track leads us away from Standedge
Cutting and soon gives way to a footpath following the escarpment
of millstone grit and crosses by the heads of two streams draining
SW, past height 1,455 ft/443 m on Cattleshaw Moor to the
Huddersfield road A640. Cross this road and follow alongside a
long wall northerly then westerly round the north side of White
Hill, 1,533 ft/466 m, then north to the Halifax road A672 near
Windy Hill television reflector station.

Windy Hill to Blackstone Edge 2 miles/3.2 km

The boundary now follows the watershed from which streams
descend on one side into Lancashire, and the other into Yorkshire.
Mile after mile of black peat and tussocky grass stretch around, vast
and uninhabited. On both sides lie two of the most densely
populated parts of the world, but these moors are as lonely as any.

These austere moorlands are of the greatest economic
importance as extensive gathering grounds for the water supply of
the neighbouring thickly populated centres on the adjacent foothills
and lowlands. The soft water running from these peat covered
moors first attracted the bleachworks and the weaving sheds, round
which the houses still cluster. Many of the mills are now closed and
are empty or converted to other uses and since the advent of the

Blackstone Edge to Wadsworth Moor

Clean Air Act the air is much cleaner, but nevertheless the smoke from the textile towns has added a tinge to the mountain grass and heather on the hills and the rocks are blackened by soot and grime.

From Windy Hill follow over rough ground along the top of Blackstone Edge as far as the Roman road.

The silence of the moors hereabouts was shattered, for a period of five years between autumn 1966 and winter 1971, by the operations of giant earth moving equipment working on the construction of the Trans-Pennine Motorway, M62. The dull roar of traffic can be heard in the deep cutting, and the road's presence is made known at night by the orange glow in the sky from the hundreds of sodium lamps that line its route.

The Pennine Way has been provided for by the construction of a graceful single-span footbridge over the motorway cutting, a three-pin arch with side cantilevers, supporting pre-stressed concrete approach spans, leaping 220 ft/67 m across the abyss. Rumour has it that the bridge was a personal whim of Ernest Marples, the then Minister of Transport and a keen rambler. After all, the interchange of M62 and A672 is not too far away, and little ingenuity would be required to divert the footpath into an underpass below one of the bridges. Fortunately the Pennine Way walker has not been relegated to a subterranean culvert, but elevated to an aerial terraceway over one of the most spectacular motorway projects in the country.

Blackstone Edge

Blackstone Edge, 'The Andes of England' as Defoe called it, towers above the smoke and dirt of industrialism. Here both Lancashire and Yorkshire fall away on either hand; Lancashire more steeply and ruggedly than Yorkshire, with long-distance views along the crest of the Pennines. Legend connects several of the summit rocks with Robin Hood, who, if ever he were here, would see one of the grandest prospects in Lancashire; towns, villages, factories, print works, dye mills and chimneys, and patches of reservoirs to supply the mills and canals.

'Then I came to Blackstone Edge,' wrote Celia Fiennes of her journey in 1698, 'noted over all England for a dismal high precipice

The 'Roman Road' over Blackstone Edge

The Pennine Way footbridge over the M62

and steep in the ascent and descent on Either End; it's a very moorish ground, all about, and Even just at the top, tho' so high, that you travel on a Causey wch is very troublesome as its a moist ground soe as is unusual on these high hills; they stagnate the aire and hold mist and raines almost perpetually.'

The Causey is marked on the maps, and always referred to as the Roman road, though archaeologists differ. The gauge of the wheel-ruts is the same as those of the roads of Pompeii and of Hadrian's Wall. With the kerbs, the road is almost 18 ft/5.5 m wide, with perfect paving and a plain camber. There is a deep groove, either cut or worn, in a line of huge stones that run down the centre of the causeway. It may have acted as a guide to a skid which was used to brake vehicles as they descended the steep incline. The road is now more or less overgrown with whortle and crowberry, but the best preserved section is found at the start of the descent into Lancashire. At the summit the road is unmistakable, and appears to have been cut through solid rock, with paving superimposed.

After you have left the gritstone outcrop of Blackstone Edge proper and continued along the boundary ridge, there will cross your path at right angles a well paved and ancient road near a cross called the Aiggin Stone.

This track now at your feet is the presumed Roman road; Roman coins have been found nearby, and certainly the Romans did have a road from Manchester to Aldburgh which must have crossed the Edge near this point.

Blackstone Edge Roman Road

Mr H. C. Collins has made a special study of the roads in this district and says: 'It is not "Roman" in pavement, although the width of the road and of the tyre marks have been compared with other Roman examples.' He continues:

'If these centre grooved troughstones have no relation to Roman roads, they certainly have very humble origins, and can be compared with any packhorse "causey" track on the Pennines, where they are the main feature. But some say that this cannot be a packhorse track because of the pavement on either side of the centre groove stones, the lateral fosses, the cut-and-cover drains, and kerbstones. The latter are referred to in Adam Watkin's *Observations* (1791), where he writes: "For many ages and to the middle of this century, a causeway, about two feet broad, paved with rounded pebbles, was all that a man or horse could travel upon, particularly in the winter season through both Lancashire and Cheshire."

'There is an example of this type of causeway only a few yards from the Roman road, which it joins at the Aiggin Stone. It has a line of centre groove stones, some of them far larger and cruder than any on the "Roman" road. It has a pebble pavement on either side and kerbstones. The "Roman" road would appear to be a development from this early structure, a widening of the pavement section so that it could take the increasing amount of traffic, including carts; a traffic growing in volume with the momentum of the Industrial Revolution. These two types of causeways—the horseways and the cartways—were in continual use.'

The Aiggin Stone is a guiding-post on the summit of the 'Roman' road at the junction of the older packhorse road. On the stone is carved a Latin cross and the initials 'I.T.' An engineers' map of 1880 gives it the name of the Aiggin Stone (gg pronounced as j). Aiggin could be a corruption of Agger, a Latin word meaning an earthwork, fortress or mound (Aggerere = to heap up) or it could also be no more than the 'Edge' or 'Edging' Stone (which rhymes with Aiggin) or summit of the pass.

Among the uncut natural rock outcrops above the road can be seen the chisel marks on blocks which the road-builders and menders almost shaped as causey stones but then abandoned because of fracture. One wayside boulder hereabouts has crude crosses carved into it, a forerunner of the more ambitiously carved and erected post such as the Aiggin Stone. Another guide-post, without markings, lies fallen on the Halifax side of the summit of the 'Roman' road.

From the Aiggin Stone our route follows the narrower causeway leading northwest. This horseway was superseded by the wider 'Roman' cartway, but was still used by the loaded limegals because the 'Roman' road was so steep—in one part about 1 in $4\frac{1}{2}$. (Limegal was a packhorse carrying exported lime from impoverished

Clitheroe; Gal is a corruption of Galloway, the Scottish district
where the sturdier of these small horses were bred.) When you
reach the Broadhead Drain, cross it and follow it northwards to a
fence and a gate, then left to some quarries and the White House
Inn on the A58 Rochdale–Halifax road above Littleborough (7
miles/11.2 km from Standedge, 30 miles/48 km from Edale). Liquid
refreshment and luncheons are available during licensed hours.

The White House Inn stands at the summit of the modern road.
The old coach road from Littleborough joins here, but it is now
overgrown with grass and signposted as a bridleway. An Act of
Parliament passed on 14 January 1734 brought to an end the use of
this road, stating, 'by reason of the nature of the soil and the
narrowness of the road in several places, and of the many heavy
carriages frequently passing, it has become so exceedingly deep and
ruinous that in winter season, and often in summer, many parts
thereof are impassable for wagons, carts, and other wheeled
carriages and very dangerous to travellers'. The same Act marked
the cut of the new road 'for repairing, and widening the road from
the town of Rochdale, in the County Palatine of Lancaster, over a
certain craggy mountain called Blackstone Edge'.

White House to Stoodley Pike 5 miles/8 km
Climb the road beyond the White House Inn and pass through the
gates on the left at the summit, along the western embankment of
Blackstone Edge Reservoir and the watershed by the Regulation
Drain, then by Light Hazzles and the farthest point of Warland
Reservoir. Some of these man-made lakes are reservoirs of drinking
water, some provide for canals, and some for great industrial
undertakings, and all are resting places for mallard and gulls.

Down to the right leads Turvin Clough, once the haunt of the
Yorkshire Coiners, led by David Hartley. Spanish coins and
Portuguese moidores were common currency in those days, and the
coiners clipped the edges of these gold coins and put them back into
circulation. With the chippings they made English sovereigns, and
they were received by sheep-keepers, bankers, mill-masters and
others at advantageous rates. In time, however, the government put
a customs officer on the track of the coiners, but he learned too

much for his safety and was killed one night by one of the gang. However, one of these gave news of Hartley's whereabouts and he was captured and later hanged at York.

On reaching the Warland Drain past the farthest reservoir turn east to a parish boundary, and continue along that line north-easterly to a wall which is followed to Stoodley Pike, an obelisk commemorating the Battle of Waterloo (5 miles/8 km from White House Inn; 35 miles/56 km from Edale).

Stoodley Pike is visible from afar, and stands 120 ft/56 m high on the top of a 1,300 ft/381 m ridge. The Pike has a faintly prophetic reputation with local people, there have been a series of collapses, replacements and repairs which were coincidental with world events.

The monument was erected to commemorate the Peace of Ghent and the abdication of Napoleon in 1814. It was finished after the Battle of Waterloo, when peace was finally established in 1815. In 1854, the day the Russian ambassador left London before the declaration of war with Russia, the Pike collapsed, and was rebuilt again when peace was declared in 1856. The cause of the collapse was thought to be erosion of the earth at the base. A lightning conductor was fixed during the first years of the Boer War, and the Pike collapsed again on the morning of 11 November 1918 just before peace was declared in World War 1.

Mankinholes

Before reaching the Pike a footpath leads down to Mankinholes from near height 1,208 ft/368 m, leaving the summit ridge at a gate in the wall we have followed from Warland Drain. Through this gateway is a carved wayside stone, with 'Te Deum Laudamus' beautifully chiselled in an old style, presumably the mark of a religious man who combined church with estate business.

The path leading down westwards to Mankinholes and the youth hostel is known as the 'Long Stoup' or the 'Long Drag' and is the easiest way off the top of the moor. It circles to ease the gradient, and is marked at intervals by tall stone pillars which act as guide posts to the track of causey stones.

The Long Drag is now partly overgrown, but in its stones lie one of the saddest stories of Lancashire—the Cotton Famine. This road was built by men whose stomachs were empty and their families starving. It is an example of how relief work was planned by a few of the best mill owners before the days of unemployment benefits.

In this case Honest John Fielden, the Unitarian philanthropist admired by Shaftesbury, provided the work of building a road to Stoodley Pike so that he could drive his private carriage to the top of the ridge from his home at Dobroyd Castle near Todmorden. It was not necessary work, but it was some return for money which he gave in terms of relief which could be called wages until the cotton mills could be reopened.

At the bottom of the steep scarp slope the track bears right towards Mankinholes village, where there is a long stone watering trough which would once serve a whole 'gang' of packhorses at a time. Mankinholes was one of the first meeting places of the Quakers, despite suppression in the reign of Charles. The earliest record of their meetings was in the house of one Joshua Laycock on 3 December 1667. They rented a croft nearby as a burial ground for 'a twopence of Silver' yearly rent for a term of 900 years. This can be traced although it is built upon. There is a gravestone in the wall of one of the buildings with the inscription 'J.S. 1685'.

Wadsworth Moor to Thornton in Craven

Stoodley Pike to Colden 5 miles/8 km
From Mankinholes to the next youth hostel at Earby is a distance of
about 20 miles/32 km, although there is accommodation at Ponden
(14 mls/22.6 km) or a diversion to the youth hostel at Howarth (17
mls/27.6 km).

Climb the flagged causey of the Long Drag from the village to the
summit ridge, then bear north to Stoodley Pike. If this monument
has already been visited, much time can be saved by taking the track
below the scarp slope to Edge End Moor, by the westerly flank of
that hill.

From Stoodley Pike a path runs east, passing a good spring after
about 200 yds/182 m, and then reaches a stile in a wall. Turn left at
the stile and follow the wall down to a track, then follow this
northerly round the east and north sides of Edge End Moor,
eventually descending to the A646 Burnley–Halifax road, the canal,
river, and railway.

This very narrow gorge of the River Calder has cotton
manufactures, clothing mills, dye works, factories and sewage
works crowded into the valley, and the smoke and smell of
industrial effluent fill the lungs. Stern terrace houses and gritstone
walls climb the side of the valley, which is an important link
between the cotton towns of Lancashire and the woollen towns of
Yorkshire.

Turn eastwards along the road for a few yards, and then left
under a railway bridge by a path that zig-zags up the steep hillside.
Looking back now we can see the outline of Stoodley Pike, two
miles/3.2 km distant.

The slope levels out, and at about 1,050 ft/315 m the Long
Causeway is crossed. This metalled road was formed during the
Middle Ages as the main traffic route between Lancashire and
Yorkshire, and it is joined throughout its length by numerous other
tracks serving all the towns in these Pennines.

The crowded life of the narrow valleys is now left behind, and
vast stretches of moorland lie beyond. The path soon drops steeply
into the valley of Colden Water near New Delight, crosses the

Stoodley Pike from the Long Drag to Mankinholes

stream by an old packhorse bridge, then climbs again to Colden and a spur of Heptonstall Moor.

Colden to Withens Height 6 miles/9.6 km

The Pennine Way from Colden bears north-westerly round height 1,284 ft/398 m on Heptonstall Moor, then northerly across the outflows from Lower Gorple and Widdop Reservoirs to the Hebden road. A turn to the right on this road will bring you to the Pack Horse Inn, and when you have refreshed yourself, retrace your steps for a distance of about half a mile/0.8 km and then turn east through an iron gate on the track to the Walshaw Dean Reservoirs, water supply for Halifax.

Cross the dam at the head of the first reservoir, then turn left beside the stone built drain. At the crossing of Black Clough follow the track north-easterly to Withens Height and Withens Farm, where there is a fresh-water spring. We have now come 10 miles/16 km from Stoodley Pike, a distance of 45 miles/72 km from Edale.

Withens Height to Ponden 3 miles/5 km

High Withens is the site Emily Brontë chose for *Wuthering Heights*, a wild spot overlooking endless miles of rolling moorland, sinister and sombre in mist and rain. These gaunt hills are immortalised by the writings of the famous Brontë sisters. The scenery of the hills is not grand nor romantic, yet it is from these hills that the sisters drew their inspiration. Charlotte once wrote: 'My sister Emily loved the moors . . . she found in the bleak solitude many and dear delights; and not the least and best loved was liberty. Liberty was the breath of Emily's nostrils; without it she perished.'

Leave Withens behind and take the track leading down to Master Stones, which then becomes a lane, but after 0.25 mile/0.4 km turn left (north) along a footpath to Buckley and Ponden Reservoir. Take the track along the south side of the reservoir, which becomes a footpath beyond Ponden Hall to Whitestone, then a lane again to the road. Ponden Hall was the Thrushcross Grange of *Wuthering Heights*. Now it provides refreshments and accommodation, and tuition in handloom weaving.

A museum dedicated to the Brontë sisters is to be found at Haworth, 3 miles/5 km to the E of Ponden, where there is also a youth hostel.

Ponden to Cowling 4 miles/6.4 km

From the Colne–Haworth road cross up Dean Fields to the higher road then bear westerly round Crag Bottom, taking the first track on the right up on to Oakworth Moor. Follow a broken wall north-westerly over Old Bess and Bare Hill on Keighley Moor, to near height 1,455 ft/443 m and a parish boundary. From this point descend northerly over Ickornshaw Moor to reach a footpath, which bears westerly to Lumb and then north to the Keighley–Colne road A6068 in Cowling village (7 miles/11.2 km from Withens; total 52 miles/83.6 km from Edale).

The Black Bull Hotel almost opposite provides refreshments. Cowling is a good place to obtain supplies, for Earby youth hostel 7 miles/11.2 km further has no store and members must cook their own meals. Alternative accommodation in this area is hard to find.

Cowling to Thornton 7 miles/11.2 km

Take the path beside the Black Bull Hotel car park, descend to the village street, pass behind some buildings to the school and follow the minor road to the hamlet of Middleton, the birthplace of Philip Snowden. A bronze plaque above the place where he was born says, 'In this cottage was born, on July 16th, 1864, the Right Honourable Philip Snowden PC, First Viscount of Ickornshaw, three times Chancellor of the Exchequer of Great Britain.' Philip Snowden was one of the brains of Ramsay MacDonald's Labour Party Government.

Beyond Gill Bridge near Middleton is a confusing series of lanes and footpaths. Turn left along the lane beside the northern bank of the stream at Gill Bridge to the ruins of an old mill, then turn right through a stile and by path uphill passing Stubbing and High Windmill farms to reach Cowling Hill Lane. Follow the road opposite steeply downhill, and at the second sharp corner enter the fields and cross the Surgill Beck, pass Woodhead Farm and then descend steeply to Lothersdale, a village where grey houses cluster about the mills by the stream. This deep valley in the heart of the moors gave the Quakers safe refuge in the times of Charles II, and Friends from afar still visit the quaint little Meeting House. The church stands high on the hillside, and beyond is Stone Gappe, the

Gateshead Hall of *Jane Eyre*. This is a fine mansion where Charlotte Brontë spent a miserable three months as governess in 1839.

In Lothersdale quite close to the Hare and Hounds will be found a Countryside Commission map and a Pennine Way signpost, which points through a farmyard to a lane. At the end of the lane the route follows field paths to Kirk Sykes and Hewitts Farms. The way now to be followed to Pinhaw Beacon is a little difficult at the beginning, and a word at either of the nearby farms may save much time and energy.

Pass through a gate at Kirk Sykes and follow a boundary wall for a short way to a stile, then strike west to Pinhaw Beacon, 1,273 ft/338 m. From the trig station on the summit descend southwest through a swathe in the heather on a line marked by cairns to an old quarry road which leads north-west to three lane ends on Elslack Moor.

Follow the Elslack road for $\frac{1}{2}$-mile/0.8 km, then bear north-westerly by Thornton Wood and Brown House to Thornton in Craven, a distance of 7 miles/11.2 km from Cowling and 59 miles/95 km from Edale.

Earby youth hostel can be reached by the footpath from the Elslack road, and this develops into a lane leading south-west to the busy little cotton town of Earby. The hostel by Wentcliff Brook was between 1922 and 1950 the home of Katherine Bruce Glasier (1867–1950), a woman who was devoted to the interests of young people and the cause of international peace. She was a pioneer of the Independent Labour Party with her husband John Bruce Glasier, a Scottish poet and designer who was a contemporary of Keir Hardie and Ramsay MacDonald and, like them, a well-known Socialist. Amond their friends were William Morris, George Bernard Shaw and H.G. Wells. The house was given by her trustees to the Association, and opened in 1958. The hostel is small and comfortable, and has attractive gardens. There are no meals provided, but there are ample facilities for self-cookers. There are shops in the town one mile/1.6 km from the hostel. Alternatively, the Manor Hotel in Thorton in Craven will provide bed and breakfast at a reasonable price.

Thornton in Craven to Malham

Thornton in Craven

The mass of millstone grit that has shaped the scenery for the last 60 miles/96.5 km now gives way to outcrops of shale and limestone. The rough moorlands and peat hags are now left behind, and pleasant footpaths lead us forward beside canal and river through dairy farming country to Malham, 11 miles/17.6 km distant.

Thornton is in a charming setting, and the 4 miles/6.4 km to Gargrave are really delightful. From the village green on the A56 road take the shaded Cam Lane northwards, which degenerates into a track to Langber Farm, but bear right on a footpath leading to the Leeds and Liverpool Canal. The towpath is followed for a short distance, and this stretch along the canal bank is at its best during the week, as at fishing season weekends it is very popular with anglers. Keep to the towpath, passing on the left the village of East Marton, where an old double-decker bridge carries the A59 over the canal. This bridge is 89 miles/143 km from Liverpool and $38\frac{1}{2}$ miles/62 km from Leeds.

Leave the canal bank $\frac{1}{4}$-mile/0.4 km beyond Williamston Bridge by a footpath which shortly regains the lane again. Follow it easterly for another $\frac{1}{4}$-mile/0.4 km, then take the field paths past Great Meadow Plantation in an almost straight line north-easterly to Scaleber and the railway cutting near Gargrave. Cross the bridge and take the footpath bearing right, emerging near the church of St Andrew by the River Aire ($4\frac{1}{2}$ miles/7.2 km from Thornton; $63\frac{1}{2}$ miles/102 km from Edale).

Gargrave

Tradition asserts that Gargrave once had seven churches, all of which were destroyed by raiding Scots except that remaining, which they spared because it was dedicated to their national saint. Other travellers who have come this way were Romans, Angles, Danes and Norsemen, for the Aire Gap was, and still is, a busy crossing through these Pennine Hills.

The road and river and the long green run side by side in this busy village. The village shops offer the last opportunities for obtaining

East Marton Bridge over the Leeds and Liverpool Canal

supplies for the next 30 miles/48 km, and meals and refreshments
are widely available.

Airedale

From Gargrave go up West Street to cross the canal on the N side of
the village, and by track and footpath over Eshton Moor. Here we
enter the Yorkshire Dales National Park. Leave the lane at the end
of the wood and climb the hill, keeping a wall on your right and trig
point on your left. At the end of the wall pass through a gate and
descend to join the River Aire by the Airton-Eshton road. Cross
the river by a footbridge and follow the west bank upstream for
$\frac{1}{2}$-mile/0.8 km to Newfield Bridge, where you cross the river again.
Climb the stile by the bridge and follow the east bank of the River
Aire to Airton and Hanlith.

Airton is a cosy little place nestling round its village green, upon
which is a squatters' house, one of the best examples still standing in
the country. In the seventeenth century when housing was difficult,
a homeless person could apply to the Quarter Sessions, who with
the consent of the township concerned, could grant him permission
to build a house with a small garden on the commons.

The Canons of Bolton Priory once had a mill here, and the old
mill by the bridge has now been converted into holiday flats.

A further $1\frac{1}{2}$ miles/2.4 km from Airton by the sparkling Aire
brings us to Hanlith, and across the river not far away is Kirkby
Malham with its interesting church. The church is most famous for
the dubious signatures of Oliver Cromwell, who witnessed a
marriage here on 17 January 1655. There is also a war memorial to
the son of Cromwell's friend, Honest John Lambert. John Lambert,
who was born at Calton Hall near Airton, helped to win the
crowning victory of the Civil War at Worcester in 1651.

Take the lane on the west bank of the river from Hanlith bridge,
which leads past an old water mill and Aire Head Springs to
Malham village, $6\frac{1}{2}$ miles/10 km from Gargrave.

Malham

Malham is an oasis in a wilderness of limestone, having many
picturesque whitewashed buildings nestling round a wide green.

The infant River Aire runs through the middle of the village and is crossed by no less than five quaint bridges. In monastic times Malham east of the beck belonged to Bolton Priory, while west of the stream was part of the Fountains Abbey estate.

Malham is an ideal place at which to spend a rest day, before we continue on the next stage of our Pennine Way journey. Some 70 miles/112 km have now been covered.

A profitable day can be spent around Malham for there are many places of interest to visit. Bed and breakfast accommodation may be obtained at the Listers Arms or the Buck Hotel or neighbouring farms, or there is the superb youth hostel. The Memorial Youth Hostel, opened in 1938, was designed by John Dower, a man who did so much for the foundation of National Parks. The Buck Hotel once had a surprising collection of big game heads, horns and antlers, but these have long been removed, along with a mosaic floor which was given by John Ruskin.

It is a tough 25 mls/40 km to the next youth hostel directly on the Pennine Way at Hawes. It is advisable to split this section into two by breaking your journey at Horton in Ribblesdale, where bed and breakfast or bunkhouse accommodation can be arranged.

Gordale Scar

Impressive Gordale Scar, 1¼ miles/2 km E of the village, should be visited whilst at Malham. The road twists and turns to Gordale Bridge, where just south of the road is the pretty fall of Janet's Foss. Turn off at the farm in the dip and follow the little beck across the fields until it swings suddenly between the towering cliffs of the defile. The approach to the Scar is impressive. The walls of the ravine shut out the sun and cast an eerie light on the scene. A stream gushes out of a square window high up in the limestone face, and cascades over fantastic rocks and rough-hewn steps, shut in by the precipitous cliffs 300 ft/91 m high. The noise of the waterfalls reverberates through this fantastic gorge. Wordsworth declared it to be one of the grandest objects in nature, while Gray admitted that, 'I stayed there not without shuddering, a quarter of an hour; and thought my trouble richly repaid for the impression which will last with life.'

The approach to Gordale Scar

The overhanging cliffs of Gordale Scar

Gordale Scar from the top of the falls

Professor Trueman, in his admirable *Geology and Scenery*, says of Gordale: 'It is probably a cavern of which the roof has collapsed. The walls are steep and mostly bare, the clean joint planes making great precipices where they cut through the massive beds; in several places the walls overhang slightly and at one point a remnant of a roof still remains. Near this is a small waterfall, for some water still flows along the surface, though the supply is much reduced owing to the fact that the greater part of the stream sinks below ground some way up the valley, to reach the surface again near the mouth of the gorge. Here then is an old cave which has lost its roof and has almost lost its water floor; the stream first passed underground to form the cave which is still represented by the gorge, and later found a still lower path. So the water is continuously being short-circuited.'

The waterfall at the head of the gorge can be climbed on the left-hand side unless the stream is in flood, and the beck followed up to Mastiles Lane, joining the road from Malham near Street Gate.

Geology and Botany of Craven

Gordale Scar and Malham Cove were caused by the vertical displacement of the Middle Craven Fault. The old beds of carboniferous limestone were thus thrust above the sea-level to form a 300 ft/91 m high wall, 40 miles/64 km long, above the younger gritstones. The cliffs were exposed to rain and river erosion; the limestone being soluble in even such a weak acid as rain water which has absorbed carbon dioxide from the atmosphere. Water sinks into the fissures of the rock and proceeds to form underground caverns and water-courses, which in turn affect the surface drainage, drawing streams down through 'swallow holes' and opening further caves. Drops of water percolating through the roofs of caverns form 'icicles' of calcium carbonate—stalactites; or falling to the floor evaporate to form stalagmites.

The underlying rock of these Craven uplands affects the soil, grass and woodland, the farming pattern and the local building materials. Heather, bilberry and bracken like the acid peat of gritstone and will not grow on limestone, but a wonderful range of flowers will grow on limestone that will not grow on the gritstone moorlands.

Commonplace flowers of spring in Craven are mountain pansies—both yellow and purple; birds e'een or mealy primrose; yellow rockrose and heartsease, cowslips and purple orchises, violets, primroses; aromatic snowy sweet cicely; canterbury bells in pale lilac spikes; blue meadow cranesbill and crimson bloody cranesbill; tiny dove foot, brookline and forgetmenots; spotted monkey musk; bistort, the pink passion dock; and Easter magiant—much used by dales-women for making of herb pudding.

Rarer flowers bloom in deep clefts of the limestone rocks—geranium robert, yellow toadflax, red valerian and harts' tongue ferns.

Malham to Birkwith

Malham Cove

Leaving Malham take the westernmost road that climbs up to Ewe
Moor. About halfway up the steep climb a path diverges from the
road through a gateway, leading to the Malham Cove. Approaching
the Cove through the pastures you can see regular mounds of rock
forming Iron Age field boundaries, whilst cultivation terraces can
be seen on the far hillside. They are not very easy to see, for the eye
is drawn continually towards the Cove.

A vast amphitheatre of cliffs is our destination; a wall of rock
which towers vertically to a height of 300 ft/91 m. A crystal clear
stream emerges from a long low arch at the base of the cliff and
threads its way through clumps of oak and alder.

At one time a river flowed from Malham Tarn on the moor above
and poured over the edge of the Cove in a single tremendous
waterfall, doubtless magnificent in time of flood. However, no
water now falls over the cliff. The stream which drains Malham
Tarn disappears underground at Water Sinks, destined to emerge at
Aire Head Springs below Malham village and not at the foot of the
Cove as many believe. Experiments have proved that the stream
from the Cove is one which disappears near a disused smelt-mill
south-west of Malham Tarn.

From the foot of the Cove scramble up the steep slopes on the
left-hand side and gain the top by a stile in the wall. Here, above the
Cove, is a vast limestone pavement, deeply fissured and dazzling
white in the sunshine, strange as mountains of the moon. This
regular pattern of joints and crevices is called by the Norse name
'grykes' and they leave between them 'clints' which have in their
depths a wonderful growth of ferns—harts' tongue fern, wood sorrel
and other plants, and stunted hawthorn bushes.

The dry river valley still remains above the Cove and this can be
followed up to Malham Tarn, but the Pennine Way footpath lies
just east of the dry valley. From the gate in the wall follow another
wall which runs at right-angles up the valley side. At a stile in the
wall turn north and cross Prior Rakes to Ha Mire Plantation.

Approach to Malham Cove

Of the dry valley Dr Raistrick in *The Face of North-West Yorkshire* says: 'The melt water from the snowfall and glaciers during and for a long time after the Ice Age was compelled to flow on the surface, as all the joints in the limestone were sealed by ice to a great depth. It was then that the dry valley was formed as the Cove was cut back as a huge waterfall. For centuries after the final disappearance of the ice the cover of boulder clay allowed some of the upland drainage to flow that way, but now the clay cover has been pierced and all the drainage goes underground.'

Malham Tarn

At Water Sinks the outlet from Malham Tarn percolates through limestone rubble adjacent to a wall, when it ought to run down the dry valley. Along here are numerous sink holes, marking the line where the impervious Silurian shales come into contact with the limestone of the Craven Fault. These shales support Malham Tarn, the highest lake in the Pennines, 1,229 ft/374 m above sea level. A blue-grey mirror on the fell tops, the 150 acre/60 ha lake is the property of the National Trust, with an abundance of fish and fresh water life.

The Pennine Way track skirts the eastern side of the Tarn and passes through the grounds of Malham Tarn House, a late Georgian style mansion occupying a commanding position overlooking the Tarn. The house was built by Walter Morrison in 1850, and here he lived for sixty-four years. A millionaire and Liberal MP—he sat in Parliament for forty years—he entertained many distinguished visitors: John Ruskin, John Stuart Mill, Charles Darwin and Charles Kingsley. Kingsley began writing *The Water Babies* while staying here, and many local places are recognisable in the novel.

The house and its 800 acre/323 ha estate was presented to the National Trust by Mrs Hutton Croft in 1946, and was subsequently leased from the Trust in 1948 by the Council for the Promotion of Field Studies, and accommodates about fifty students. This is now a wonderful centre for natural history students, ornithologists, botanists, and geologists. Flowers and mosses grow here which are found nowhere else in England, so please do not trespass.

The cliffs of Malham Cove

Limestone clints above the Cove

The dry valley above the Cove

Malham Tarn House

Fountains Fell

Tennant Gill

Stanggill Barn

Fountains Fell from Malham Moor

Malham Tarn to Fountains Fell 3 miles/4.8 km
Pass Malham Tarn House by the drive to Water Houses and turn
northwards on a footpath over Malham Moor. After ½-mile/0.8 km
the track is blocked by a stone wall, but follow this wall north-
easterly, crossing two other walls to reach a gate on a cart track near
Stanggill Barn. Turn left through this gate to the Arncliffe road,
which follow north for a short distance, then take the track bearing
left to Tennant Gill Farm.

An old mine track leads from the farm and ascends Fountains
Fell. This track is not very clear, and the beacons are not very good.
In bad weather take a compass bearing north-west from Tennant
Gill and this will lead you to Dale Head House. At about 1,650 ft/
503 m the track crosses the Tennant Gill and bears north, and you
can notice the transition from limestone turf to the tussocky grass of
an acid gritstone moor. There are many shake-holes and streams at
this level, but the going improves as you reach higher ground.

The gritstone lies like a cap on these mountains of limestone, and
causes them to be hollow inside with caves and potholes. In the rock
strata are thin seams of coal, and the track we are following climbs
to an outcrop on the summit of Fountains Fell.

Fountains Fell to Penyghent 4 miles/6.4 km
On the north side of the fell the track bends westerly then south-
westerly, leading down to the Silverdale Road at Dale Head.
Stainforth is some 3½ miles/5.6 km down this road to the south.
There is a youth hostel just south of the village, and the Craven
Heifer Inn in Stainforth offers accommodation and meals. The
youth hostel was built about 1848 and purchased by the Association
in 1944. In the garden are to be seen a number of bee-boles—
cavities in the thick stone wall to hold bee hives.

If you stay at the hostel here do not fail to see the old one-arch
bridge, a fine relic of packhorse days, which spans the River Ribble
in one gracious sweep. This 400-year-old bridge was formerly on the
line of an ancient track, considered the shortest route between York
and Lancaster. It has belonged to the National Trust since 1931.
While at Stainforth do not fail to see Stainforth Force to the south
of the bridge and also Catrigg Force, a fine cataract in a narrow
gorge approached up a stoney lane leading east from the village.

Since leaving Fountains Fell, Penyghent, 2,273 ft/694 m, has dominated the view, and from Dale Head Farm we commence its ascent.

From the farm a track leads to Churn Milk Hole, a notable depression on the left of the track where a small stream emerges and sinks. Though only a small cave, its boulders are loose and dangerous.

Leave the track by the pothole and continue forward to a wall, and follow this up the sheer gritstone crags to Penyghent summit cairn—a steep climb. From the breezy top—Penyghent means 'Hill of the Winds'— can be seen bare hills and miles of open country. Fountains Fell dominates the southern scene, while flat-topped Ingleborough lies due west, with Whernside and other lofty moors beyond.

Penyghent is a mass of limestone capped by a slab of millstone grit, and it is this which forms the crags around the hill. The screes of these crags are deep channels in the side of the hill; they began to appear after a cloudburst about 1930, and are now 10 ft/3 m deep and 20 ft/6 m wide. Many furious storms have caused the base of Penyghent to be honeycombed by hidden passages and waterworn channels, while in a bad winter snowdrifts may form on the top to a depth of 30 ft/9 m and remain until June.

The three peaks of Penyghent, 2,273 ft/694 m, Ingleborough, 2,373 ft/723 m, and Whernside, 2,419 ft/736 m, dominate the Pennine scene, and they seem to challenge the human spirit. The walk that encompasses all their summits is a classic of its kind. It was first recorded as being done by two school teachers on a fine night in July 1887, a distance of 27 miles/43 km in 10 hours. There is now an annual race over these fells, always on the last Sunday in April, the fastest circuit being 2 hrs 29 mins 53 secs set by Jeff Norman in 1974. Norman succeeded after 8 years to become the first athlete to break $2\frac{1}{2}$ hours for the course, and his 1974 title was his sixth successive win for the event.

Penyghent to Horton 3 miles/4.8 km
Our route follows the wall along the summit ridge north towards Plover Hill. It is difficult to find shelter on these raking slopes, and

Hunt Pot, on the flank of Penyghent

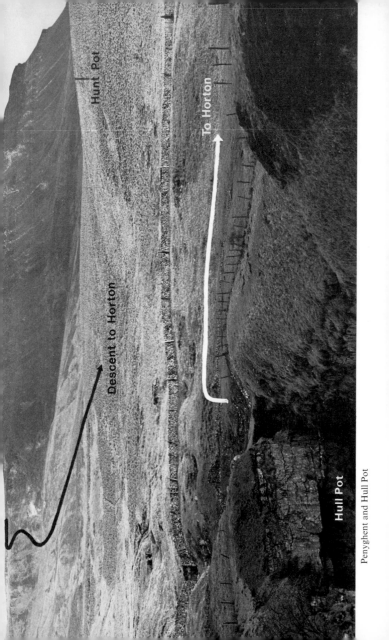

Hunt Pot

Descent to Horton

To Horton

Hull Pot

Penyghent and Hull Pot

The descent to Horton in Ribblesdale from Hull Pot

Penyghent from the green lane to Horton

the drystone walls are no help, for they were built to allow the wind to blow through their chinks instead of knocking them down.

The 4 mile/6.4 km descent to Horton starts at the saddle between Penyghent and Plover Hill by an old miners' track leading down Penyghent Side and, though steep, the descent is not difficult.

There are many potholes along this side of Penyghent which vary in depth from 60 ft/18 m to 210 ft/60 m. They are classed as very difficult, severe, and super-severe, and no exploration of them should be undertaken without proper equipment and experienced guides.

Descend the miners' track, pass through a fell gate, turn left, and then through another gate where a path leads past Hunt Pot, a narrow rift 15 ft × 6 ft × 200 ft (4.5 m × 1.8 m × 60 m) deep. In a short distance the path passes through another wicket gate and reaches a stone hut. A short distance upstream, circled by a wire fence, is the tremendous cavity of Hull Pot, 'like the inside of a great Gothic castle, the high ruinous walls of which were left standing after the roof had fallen in'. It is 300 ft long, 60 ft wide and 60 ft deep (90 m × 18 m × 18m).

The beck that feeds this pothole mostly disappears underground before it reaches the rim of the cavity, and the subdued rumblings of the hidden beck can be heard. In times of heavy rainfall the stream overflows the crack in its limestone bed and then falls into the Pot over the rim, the volume being too great to flow underground. If the rainstorm continues for an exceptional length of time the Pot fills right to the brim and many even 'boil over', then it will suddenly empty like a bathtub.

In ordinary times the Hull Pot stream emerges from a huge cave at the foot of Douk Ghyll Scar a mile/1.6 km distant, and when the Pot 'boils over' the overflow runs down the hollows to fall over the Scar in a thin and slender cascade.

From the gate near Hull Pot a rough walled-in green lane descends gradually to Horton in Ribblesdale, 2 miles/3.2 km away (14 miles/22.5 km from Malham: total 84 miles/135 km).

Horton in Ribblesdale

Horton is a little place of whitewashed and sombre grey cottages haphazardly sited round a stream which feeds the Ribble. The charming little church is a focal point, to which we are led by two quaint lych gates, each with a roof made of two great stone slabs.

The church of St Oswald still retains many primitive Norman features, though it was restored in 1400 when the sturdy perpendicular west tower was added. The Norman nave chancel and aisles are all under one roof, whose leaded covering was obtained from the mining of crude ore from Hull Pot. In the west window of the tower is a fragment of stained glass showing the mitred head of Thomas à Becket, whose murder was news when the church was young. On the glass are the words 'Thomas Cantaur'.

Horton has a good inn, The Crown, while the Penyghent Café between the inn and the church provides good meals and refreshments. The Café owners will also be able to direct the walker to local bed and breakfast or bunkhouse accommodation and a camp site in the village.

Horton to Hawes 14 miles/22.5 km

The Pennine Way route from Horton into Wensleydale starts out on the green lane from the Crown Inn (marked New Inn on the map) leading north, passing Sell Gill Holes after one mile/1.6 km. A natural bridge divides the two entrances to this pothole, which is 210 ft/64 m deep. A little farther north lies Jackdaw Hole, where trees fringe a 70 ft × 40 ft/21 m × 12 m opening.

The green lane is followed on to Birkwith Moor, where the official route is rather complex to follow until Old Ing Farm is reached. Leave the green lane at a gate in a wall, go westerly over a low hill to a barn, then follow a wall to a track which leads to Old Ing.

Old Ing will be the start of the possible line of a proposed long-distance footpath link from the Pennine Way to the Lake District. This will give walkers the opportunity of proceeding to the Lakes by way of a scenic footpath as an alternative to continuing northwards to the Roman Wall and the Cheviots.

From Old Ing another green lane, an old packhorse track, leads round the side of Cave Hill to Cam Beck. Two hundred yards/182 m north of Old Ing Farm beside this lane is Dry Laithe Cave, with a 35 ft/10.6 m deep entrance shaft down which a stream falls, to emerge

Penyghent, from Horton in Ribblesdale

Plover Hill

Crown Inn

◀To Sell Gill Holes

To Ribblehead ▶

Penyghent and the Crown Inn, Horton in Ribblesdale

The green lane from Horton to Birkwith Moor

Birkwith to Hawes

at the large opening of Browgill Cave ¼-mile/0.4 km westwards.

The track leads towards Cam Beck and the ravine of Ling Gill. The Gill is a collapsed cave, and great crags reach to a height of nearly 300 ft/91 m, whilst its bed is strewn with blocks and boulders of every size and shape. In midwinter icicles like organ pipes hang from the cliffs and the Gill holds a terrifying silence. In summer it is enchanting; rowans and rock-held hollies catch the sun and ledges are gay with foxgloves, harebells and sheep-bit scabious, and the air is loud with singing birds.

Ling Gill is crossed by a famous bridge, built of grit quarried from the Cam Beck course. It was originally built for the benefit of travellers on the main pre-turnpike road from Settle to Hawes, and a stone tablet records in quaint lettering: 'Anno 1765 (or 68). This bridge was repaired at the charge of the whole West Ridinge.'

From Ling Gill Bridge an easy path leads down the right hand side of the Gill, in places nearly 200 ft/60 m above the stream bed, and even the stream bed itself with its fine waterfall can be followed with care.

From Cam Beck go forward along a mile of rough track to reach a Roman road at Cam End, 1,432 ft/436 m, and bear north over Cam Fell. This Roman road leading to Bainbridge in Wensleydale was once called the Devil's Causeway—a belief that no human hands could have engineered such a road so well, enduring for so long. In the Middle Ages men feared nightfall on the Cam. They hastened onwards, glad to hear the sound of Bainbridge's horn carried to them on the wind. Wolves ranged the tops, and the hornblower sounded the alarm as a warning for all to bring down flocks and herds to safety.

Two miles/3.2 km further along the Roman road the remote farm of Cam Houses appears in a lonely dip. Not far beyond is the watershed of England where the head streams of the Wharfe and Ribble are separated by a patch of hilltop.

We leave the Roman road near Dodd Fell at height 1,877 ft/ 572 m on an old green track north-easterly alongside Dodd Fell. From this junction there is a marvellous view of hill and dale, and, looking back, the flat top of Ingleborough, 7½ miles/12 km distant.

Dry Laithe Cave, near Horton Ribblesdale

Ling Gill Bridge

Gayle and the Duerley Beck, near Hawes, Wensleydale

Great Shunner Fell

Hardrow Force

Footpath to Gayle ▼

Hardrow and Great Shunner Fell from Hawes, Wensleydale

Our track continues to Hawes over the steep shoulder of Dodd Fell to Ten End, then by footpath to Backsides, Gaudy House and Gayle. The Ten End—Backsides footpath offshoot is not clear, and is difficult to find in mist.

Gayle is an unusual little village, with old stone houses and barns standing higgledy-piggledy in narrow twisting streets. The wide stream which cascades over broad rocky ledges through the village is the home of a considerable floating population of geese, and in dry weather children use the beck as their playground.

Wensleydale

Do not cross the bridge but take the road to Hawes, and after a few hundred yards/metres take the churchyard path on the right-hand side, which delivers you suddenly into the midst of this busy market town (14 miles/22.5 km from Horton; 98 miles/157 km from Edale).

Hawes, in Wensleydale, is one of the highest market towns in the country, and is famous for its waterfalls and dairy cheese. Its grey rugged houses and inns huddle round a cobbled main street, which is where the market and sheep sales are held every Tuesday.

Hawes is an ideal place for bed and breakfast accommodation, whether in the good inns or in private houses. It is also a good centre for supplies (early closing day Wednesday) as the next good place for supplies is 4 or 5 days' march away at Alston. The Yorkshire Dales National Park Planning Committee has constructed a youth hostel in Hawes which is operated on similar lines to those at Crowden and Once Brewed. (This youth hostel is 22 miles/35 km from the hostel at Stainforth, but only 8 miles/12.8 km from Dentdale hostel, although Dentdale is 20 miles/32 km from Stainforth if you follow the Way over Penyghent. Keld hostel is 12 miles/19 km from Hawes along the Pennine Way.)

The Dales Countryside Museum is well worth a visit whilst you are in Hawes. It contains a remarkable collection of farming and other artefacts built up by local historians and authors Marie Hartley and Joan Ingleby. The museum incorporates the Dales National Park Centre and is housed in former station buildings on the long-since-closed Wensleydale Railway. The Pennine Way passes its door.

Hawes to Tan Hill

Wensleydale to Swaledale 10 miles/16 km
From Hawes take the road to Hardrow, crossing the disused railway
by the Countryside Museum, then north to the bridge over the River
Ure by the riverside pastures. Once across the river keep to the road
for a short distance and up the hill. Above the spinney leave the road,
climb a stile on the left hand side and cross the golf course by a
footpath that leads into the tiny hamlet of Hardrow.

Here a cluster of grey houses stand round a fine old bridge, but
the main attraction is the Hardrow Force, approached through the
parlour of the Green Dragon Inn for a small fee. The walk to the
falls leads up a wooded ravine noted for its acoustic properties, a
place where brass band contests were held in Victorian days. This
tradition has been revived in recent years, and events cause serious
traffic congestion in the valley.

The fall lies at the head of a deep cleft in the hills, plunging over a
projecting shelf of rock in an uninterrupted drop of nearly 100 ft/
30 m. The fall is one of the most graceful in the country, and you can
walk behind it and look through it, to see the sun falling on the
silver shower with the glory of a thousand rainbows. Turner thought
it wonderful enough to paint, and both Wordsworth and Ruskin
were captivated by it. That indefatigable tourist, Doctor Richard
Pococke, visited and described these Wensleydale falls in 1751, and
he recorded that in the great frost of 1739–40 Hardrow Force froze
into a single hollow column measuring $72\frac{3}{4}$ yds/66.5 m in
circumference.

Leave Hardrow at the west end of the village and turn north on a
green lane by the school, and follow this old mine track up the spur
of Great Shunner Fell. Shunner is ascended by a footpath following
the line of beacons over Black Hill Moss and Jinglemea Crag, past
old coal pits and lead mines. The 2,340 ft/716 m summit is a long
way off, but the route is not difficult to find even in heavy mist if use
is made of careful compass readings and constant observation of the
beacons.

From the summit traverse north-east past a beacon, keeping to
the ridge on the north side of Stock Dale, dropping down to join an
old road leading to Thwaite in Swaledale.

Hardrow Force

◄ To Thwaite   ▲ To Moor Close Farm and Stock Dale   B 6270   To Keld ►

Great Shunner Fell, from near Thwaite, Swaledale

Thwaite in Swaledale

Kisdon Hill

Doctor Wood

To Thwaite

Kisdon Hill from Thwaite

Kisdon Force, near Keld, Swaledale

Swaledale

Thwaite is a strange little village, where stone houses and walls merge into the landscape, and it was here that the famous brothers Richard and Cherry Kearton were born. The sons of a gamekeeper, they were born naturalists and acquired their intimate knowledge of wild life as boys on these moorlands. Richard was crippled during his early years, and this helped to foster his natural gifts. It was during a shooting party on the moors that Richard attracted the attention of Mr Cassell, the London publisher, and he entered the latter's London office where his wonderful gifts were quickly recognised. Richard won fame as a naturalist and lecturer, while Cherry Kearton, who followed his brother to London, became famous as a pioneer of wild life photography. The two brothers collaborated in many books, and their work revolutionised the study of wild life at close quarters.

Teas are provided at the Kearton Guest House in the village of Thwaite, while the Queens and Farmers Arms in neighbouring Muker, where the Kearton brothers attended school, are able to provide bed and breakfast accommodation. There is a youth hostel at Keld, 3 miles/4.8 km further on our journey.

From Thwaite the Pennine Way climbs up Kisdon Hill, 1,636 ft/499 m, crossing the old corpse track that climbs from Muker by Kisdon Farm. This section of the route over Kisdon presents many difficulties, and problems in misty weather, and is not satisfactorily defined. The signpost in Thwaite village is really misleading, as it directs one to the Muker road. Local people do not admit the officially approved route to be a right of way.

The path crosses the east side of Kisdon Hill, descending to Kisdon Force, where the young Swale tumbles 30 ft/9 m into a rocky glen. The path to Keld village and the youth hostel climbs the bank side again, while the Pennine Way route crosses the Swale by footbridge on its way to Tan Hill.

Keld, 12 miles/19.2 km from Hawes, 110 miles/176 km from Edale, is a fascinating hamlet of grey houses. The youth hostel, above the hamlet on the Kirkby Stephen road, was formerly a shooting lodge, but its austere appearance belies its friendly atmosphere. The hostel is very well patronised because Keld is also

Keld, Swaledale, from the Youth Hostel

where the Pennine Way is crossed by the Coast to Coast Path. From the hostel at Keld to the next one at Baldersdale is 15 miles/24 km, a convenient day's walk. The alternative is to use bed and breakfast accommodation in Barnard Castle, a few miles/km east of the route, or Middleton in Teesdale 21 miles/33.6 km further on, or to camp.

Keld to Stainmore 10 miles/16 km

Leave Keld and follow the path down to the Swale, and cross by the footbridge to East Stonesdale and Shot Lathe, then by an old road over Stonesdale Moor to the Tan Hill Inn. The track, though indistinct, is well cairned from Lad Gill to Tan Hill.

Tan Hill Inn is undoubtedly the highest licensed house in England. It is situated in an exposed and most desolate spot, 1,732 ft/528 m above sea level. It is dwarfed into insignificance by the loneliness of its surroundings, wild moorland stretching as far as the eye can see in every direction.

The inn was built for the refreshment of miners who lived in bothies or 'shops' near the local workings and returned to their Swaledale homes at the weekends, and also for the carters who carried away the minerals. The coal workings, in shallow seams 4 ft/1.2 m thick, are now no longer worked.

From Tan Hill we leave the Yorkshire Dales National Park and descend north-easterly on a cairned route down Frumming Beck to Sleightholme Beck, and then along a track to Sleightholme Farm. In wet weather avoid Frumming Beck, and instead walk east along the Arkengarthdale road as far as Cocker, and then by a semi-metalled track leading to Sleightholme Farm.

A little beyond Sleightholme take the path which crosses the Beck by a footbridge, and follow a wall leading to Trough Heads Farm, where the Bowes bad-weather route diverges.

The footpath from Trough Heads over Wytham Moor to West Mellwaters is easy to follow, and leads to God's Bridge over the River Greta. At this point we are nearly halfway to Scotland, being 120 miles/193 km from Edale. God's Bridge is a curious natural limestone bridge spanning the river, and except at floodtime the Greta flows underground at this point. The river caves under God's Bridge extend to over 3,000 ft/914 m and provide some very sporting and severe caving for experts in the sport.

Tan Hill to Lunedale

Sleightholme Beck

The Pennine Way near Sleightholme, Stainmore Forest

God's Bridge, spanning the River Greta in Stainmore Gap

From God's Bridge pass between the abutments of a demolished railway bridge and follow a rough track which ascends to a gate beside the very busy Bowes–Brough road, route A66.

Alternative Route: Bowes Loop 8 miles/12 km
This diversion is only 3 miles/4.8 km longer than the main Way, yet it avoids the crossing of the Bowes and Cotherstone Moors in bad weather.

From Trough Heads follow the Sleightholme Beck by East Mellwaters and Lady Mires to Bowes. Bowes was one of two Roman forts controlling the Stainmore crossing, but it is today remembered chiefly because Dickens made it the scene of 'Dotheboys Hall' in *Nicholas Nickleby*. A social conscience inspired Dickens to protest against the bad old Yorkshire schools where boys suffered at the hands of masters such as Wackford Squeers. Much feeling was aroused by this picture, and great improvements resulted.

Dotheboys Hall is now a transport café. West End Farm and Clint Farm provide overnight accommodation. To reach the youth hostel at Barnard Castle necessitates 5 miles/8 km of main road walking or using an infrequent bus service. The new youth hostel at Baldersdale is 5 miles/8 km further along the way.

Leaves Bowes at the western end of the village and pass between the abutments of an old railway bridge on a track which leads north-west to Tute Hill and Levy Pool by Deepdale Beck. Cross Ministry of Defence land by footpaths west of Loup's Plantation to Yawd Sike and Friar House, then west to rejoin the main route at Clove Lodge Farm at the head of Baldersdale Reservoir.

Main Route:
Stainmore to Baldersdale 5 miles/8 km
Stainmore is a vital Pennine crossing and the first major one since we left the Aire Gap at Gargrave. After the M62 the A66 is perhaps the busiest trans-Pennine road we cross. Unlike the M62, however, there is no footbridge to cross this busy road. The Department of Transport plans to widen the A66 here to dual-carriageway standard, but they have so far rejected pleas for a footbridge to take

Mickle Fell

Deepdale Beck

Ravock Castle on Bowes Moor

Pennine Wayfarers safely over the busy road. We leave the main road at Pasture End and head north beside the enclosure wall west of the farm, striking out over Bowes Moor to the highest point of the ridge. Bear north-westerly following the line of cairns to Ravock Castle, a ruined shepherd's hut. Ahead lies a vast region of treeless and swampy moorland. The country is deeply indented and broken by innumerable becks, so that crossing it is not easy, though much of the ground is good. Flat-topped Shacklesborough Moss, 1,489 ft/ 454 m, on Cotherstone Moor is a good landmark in this featureless country.

Descend to the Deepdale Beck and follow a path north running parallel to the line of an enclosure wall which is the western boundary of Ministry of Defence land, and head for a dip on the horizon. Beyond this dip, at the summit of the next ridge, stands an old boundary stone known as Race Yate at a height of 1,402 ft/ 427 m. It carries the date 1729 and marks the division of the moors of Bowes and Cotherstone. From this point there is a gradual descent by height 1,247 ft/338 m on Cotherstone Moor to the head of Baldersdale at Clove Lodge Farm. The former Blackton Farm has been converted into a youth hostel, conveniently splitting the 30 miles/48 km between Keld and Langdon Beck into two equal lengths.

The River Balder has been impounded by dams to form reservoirs for the Tees Valley Water Board, and like those in neighbouring Lunedale, they add an element of interest to these bleak little valleys.

Baldersdale to Lunedale 3 miles/4.8 km
Take the track from Clove Lodge and the youth hostel through Birk Hat to High Birk Hat and the Hunderthwaite road, then by footpath beside an enclosure wall over Hazelgarth Rigg and Mickleton Moor to How in Lunedale and the Grassholme Reservoir.

Lunedale to Teesdale 3 miles/4.8 km
Cross the bridge over the reservoir and then from beside the first barn near Grassholme farm make a straight line northwards

Baldersdale, from height 1,247 ft on Cotherstone Moor

through fields to the Mickleton-Brough road, B6276. Cross this road and beside a barn take the track leading round Wythes Hill, then turn east on a path crossing several fields above the old quarries to height 1,577 ft/481 m on Harter Fell. From here descend gradually north-easterly past two small reservoirs to reach the road B6277 near a camping and caravan area on the site of the former Middleton station. Another half mile/0.8 km brings us into Middleton in Teesdale, 20 miles/32 km from Keld, 130 miles/209 km from Edale. Langdon Beck youth hostel lies 8 miles/12.8 km farther upstream on the River Tees.

Lunedale, from Mickleton Moor

Middleton in Teesdale

Middleton was once the centre of a flourishing lead-mining industry. In 1652 William and Mary granted a charter to the London Lead Company, whose operations were finally abandoned in 1905 owing to the low price of the metal and the decreasing percentage of silver in it, which rendered the business unprofitable. The Quakers who ran the Company looked after their work-people well, providing a school, chapels, a library and substantial cottages. A solid looking stone building with a clock tower, set among tall trees overlooking the little town, was built about 1820 as the head office of the Company; now it is used as an hotel.

The church of St Mary was rebuilt about 1866, and has the only example of a detached belfry in Durham. It is a low structure in the north wall of the churchyard and was built in 1557. Also in the churchyard near the gate are the steps of the old market cross, now supporting a sundial on a round stone shaft; an iron band on the lower step is a relic of the stocks.

In the village is the Bainbridge Memorial Fountain of 1877, an ornamental cast iron canopy with the figure of a child, still much in the 1851 taste.

Teesdale Geology

Both the lead mining which made Middleton important and the scenery which brings visitors to Upper Teesdale are aspects of the earth's crust which over wide stretches of this countryside now provide the prominent interest.

The structure of this portion of the Pennines, which extends from Stainmore to the Tyne valley, is comparatively simple. The sharp western slope, along the line through Cross Fell, and reaching more than 2,000 ft/608 m above sea level, forms a great scarp, along a fault which brings the new red sandstone of the Eden valley into contact with the older rocks of the moors. From the steep western escarpment the desolate moorland and bleak pasture slope gradually away to the east, sinking almost imperceptibly to the plains of the Durham coalfield.

The strange romantic scenery of Upper Teesdale, with its great waterfalls and black scars, is due to the intrusion of igneous rock known as the Whin Sill. The Whin Sill was injected molten into the orderly strata of the carboniferous series and bares itself at Holwick Scars, the crags of Cronkley, Falcon Clints and the gorge of High Cup Nick; it gives the river its most turbulent stretches and forms the two great waterfalls of High Force and Cauldron Snout, and it also forms the crags along the line of the Roman Wall.

Middleton to High Force 4 miles/6.4 km

From Middleton, near the cattle pens just short of the bridge over the Tees, on the Yorkshire (west) side, take a lane leading north-west, which eventually becomes a footpath on the bank of the river.

This riverside footpath is now followed for many miles/ kilometres, and hedgerows and meadows make this a very pleasant walk. Three miles/4.8 km from Middleton we come to Winch Bridge, picturesquely placed amid hazel woods shading a narrow gorge.

This unusual suspension bridge spanning the Tees where it swirls through a ravine was originally built by miners in 1704, and claimed to be the earliest suspension bridge in England. It was composed of two main chains 70 ft/21 m long, with 2 ft/0.6 m planks laid across, a handrail only on one side and hung 20 ft/6 m above the river. It was damaged by the great flood of 1771 but was quickly repaired.

Hutchinson in his *History of Durham* of 1794 says that it was used principally by miners, 'a restless gangway to which few strangers dare trust themselves'. The miners lived in Holwick and worked in the lead mines in the fells above Newbiggin. The bridge collapsed in 1820 while nine men were crossing, one falling to the narrow rocky gorge below and losing his life. The present structure dates from 1830, and was washed by the river in times of severe flood before the construction of Cow Green reservoir.

Immediately above Winch Bridge the country is more open, and the river comes down over a wide stretch of black basalt in torrents of rusty foam, to form glittering cascades and placid pools. This is Low Force, and the falls are divided by a delightful wooded island called Staple Crag, an upstanding mass of detached rock where gorse and heather grow.

The Tees Bridge. Middleton in Teesdale

Winch Bridge near Newbiggin

The Tees at Low Force, above Winch Bridge

Upstream of Low Force the strange basaltic river bed forms the pleasant cascade of Holwick Force, where the impetuous river flows in a deeply cut glen.

We have now been following the Tees for some 4 miles/6.4 km through meadow land and rough pasture, over a large assortment of stiles, along overgrown paths, and past some of the most varied stretches of this ever changing dale. The eroded columns and dykes of Whin Sill which lie across the bed deflect the water into a maze of channels, pools and cataracts, into which the angler casts his fly in search of the brown trout.

If you have kept to the right bank (Yorkshire side) of the river, you don't have to cross the wooden bridge which leads to Holwick Head House. From here we leave the river level and start to climb the high bank over the Tees gorge, on our approach to High Force.

By the gate-way in the fence at the top of this climb is a Pennine Way notice and a map marking the boundary to the Teesdale Nature Reserve.

Six thousand five hundred acres/2 630 ha of Upper Teesdale were declared a National Nature Reserve in September 1963, the second largest in the country. It is bounded on the north by the River Tees and on the south by Mickle Fell, and on the west by the county boundary. North of Dufton Fell it adjoins the 10,000 acres/4 047 ha of the Moor House National Nature Reserve, which the Nature Conservancy Council established in 1952.

The main objects of the reserve are to extend the important researches of highland Britain and those on water conservation which are in progress at Moor House, as well as to safeguard the flora and fauna of Upper Teesdale.

Beyond the gate the path leads through a maze of juniper thickets, and passes very close to the edge of the gorge in several places, giving occasional glimpses of the High Force.

High Force is the finest waterfall in England. The River Tees, after many upland miles of open moor, comes tumbling down a wide rocky channel of Whin Sill, and suddenly leaps 70 ft/21 m into the abyss below, forming a deep swirling pool almost as deep. The vast amphitheatre is bounded by grim walls of black basalt with vertical joints resting on horizontal layers of mountain limestone.

High Force

High Force

A mighty rock divides the stream in two, though normally the fall on the Durham side is little more than a trickle. At ordinary seasons it is easily possible to scramble on to the top of the central rock, and look down into the chasm below. Even in moderate flow the main fall looks impressive, and on rare occasions of cloudbursts or exceptional floods the central rock is covered, creating an enormous fall 100 ft/30 m high. The thunder of the Force when the Tees is in spate is deafening, and can be heard for a considerable distance.

> Filled was the air with music true
> Though loved, alas! by far too few.
> For nature's sounds are sweet to hear
> If listened for by trained ear.
> The Tees itself, though far away
> Threading its course through distance grey,
> Proclaims aloud with a mighty roll
> Its progress to a far-off goal;
> And rushing madly headlong o'er,
> At High Force leaps with a ceaseless roar.
> Thence bubbling, hissing, onward goes
> Till lost to view in deep repose.
>
> Sir Walter Scott

High Force to Langdon Beck 3 miles/4.8 km
The High Force can also be approached from the Middleton road on the Durham bank, where a footpath descends through the heavily wooded gorge from the High Force Hotel, a discarded shooting lodge of the Dukes of Sutherland. However, the Pennine Way follows the best approach, on the Yorkshire bank, and visitors also avoid paying the toll to the Raby Estates.

Above the Force the path still continues on the Yorkshire bank, threading its way through a miniature forest of juniper bushes. The juniper is a sturdy, evergreen shrub with thickly spreading branches, and its bluish-green contrasts pleasantly with the changing colours of the bracken. Chips of juniper wood were used for fumigating houses in times of sickness or plague, and the berries are used for flavouring gin.

The Tees above High Force

Opposite the Blea Beck crossing is a whinstone quarry, the ugly stone-crushing machinery striking a jarring note in this wild scene. Further upstream the footpath reaches Skyer Beck. The route then bears north to Cronkley Farm and a bridge over the Tees.

Descending to this bridge we get a glimpse of the bare, treeless fells, the monotony broken by whitewashed farmhouses. The tale is told that a former Lord Barnard had to seek shelter in a farmhouse overnight, and for this kindness he told the farmer to have all the repairs done and the bill sent to his estate agent. When a heavy bill arrived the agent pointed out to a surprised Lord Barnard that the farm was not part of his estate, and consequently his lordship ordered all farms on his estate to be whitewashed annually.

The Tees bridge is crossed and the river followed upstream on the Durham bank, and at the confluence follows the Langdon Beck to the next bridge near New House Farm. At this point the Langdon Beck youth hostel may be easily reached, a distance of 8 miles/12.8 km from Middleton, 138 miles/222 km from Edale.

Langdon Beck Youth Hostel is ideally situated for the next stage of our journey, for from here it is some 15 miles/24 km to the next hostel in the Vale of Eden. This hostel replaces one on the same site which was destroyed by fire in November 1958. There is excellent accommodation, with hot showers, a drying room and meals provided to take care of the rain-soaked and hungry traveller. Alternatively meals may be obtained from the Langdon Beck Hotel one mile/1.6 km distant.

Upper Teesdale to Vale of Eden 12 miles/19.2 km
From the bridge over the Langdon Beck near New Houses a footpath leads westerly to Widdybank Farm, though the route is rather vague.

Widdybank Fell was so named because here an outcrop of soft slate was once worked for the making of slate pencils, known in the district as 'Widdies'. Near the farm is an old ruined pencil mill.

The path now follows Holmwath, the pastures beside the Tees which are rich in wild flowers. Unique soil and climatic conditions for alpine plants found here in Upper Teesdale do not seem to be present anywhere else in the country. Outcrops of 'sugar' limestone

weather to give a lime-rich granular soil, and in such places many of
the Teesdale rarities grow. Most abundant of these flowers are the
stone violet and the bird's eye primrose, while yellow saxifrage and
shrubby cinquefoil grow in plenty in the damp patches beside the
river. Much more elusive are the white bog sandwort and the little
blue spring gentian, but there are many other commoner flowers—
violets, primroses and wild pansies.

The Tees swings round the foot of the high dark cliffs of Cronkley
Scar in a shallow and stony channel, and the scene increases with
magnificence as we approach Falcon Clints along the path which
winds its way on the river bank. Great grey cliffs rise from a
foundation of heather and bilberry tufts, and soon we are at the
junction of the Tees and the Maize Beck — the meeting place of
Yorkshire, Durham and Cumbria.

A few yards/metres away northwards is Cauldron Snout, where
the Tees falls 200 ft/60 m in 150 yds/137 m, the Whin Sill forming a
tremendous series of cataracts. Approaching from below you turn
suddenly to face the stairway of the fall at the level of the agitated
surface of the cauldron. The water pours into this pool in a white
foam over the snout which forms the final step of the descent, and
high above you see its first leap from the skyline.

It is an easy scramble up the natural rocky stairway on the eastern
bank, from which you can observe the fall in all its grandeur. The
view from the top of the fall is the extensive spread of moorland
rimmed by distant fells, whose lower slopes are possibly dark below
white mists that rake their tops.

Above Cauldron Snout the Tees once threaded its way through a
tract of extreme desolation, during which it hardly seemed to flow,
in the long, level expanse of the Weil, but now it has stopped
flowing altogether as it runs into Cow Green Reservoir. Against a
background of amenity value, scientific study and conservation,
proposals to establish a reservoir at Cow Green excited and
stimulated considerable opposition when the Tees Valley &
Cleveland Water Board promoted a Bill in 1967 to control the
abstraction of water from the River Tees primarily to serve the ICI
plant at Billingham. The reservoir was 'opened' on 22 July 1971.

At a cost of £2½m 770 acres/311 ha of land were flooded to a

Falcon Clints

The Tees at Cauldron Snout

maximum depth of 75 ft/22 m to contain 9,000 million gallons/
40 914 million litres of water. The 82ft/25 m high dam, 623 yds/570
m long, dominates the head of Cauldron Snout. The fate of this fine
mountain cataract, and that of High Force, depend on the volume
of water the engineers permit to escape through the sluices. It is the
intention to regulate the flow of the river at times of high flow, but
in dry weather compensation water will be released to increase
normal dry weather flows.

It was argued that the reservoir would do irreparable damage to
the cause of conservation by flooding an area of unique botanical
interest. Rare plant communities, relics of a tundra vegetation and
considered to be of unique quality, grow in this area, and are of
importance for long-term biological research. These plant
communities grow on limestone soils derived from the sugar
limestone which lies above the Whin Sill over this area. Every effort
was made to cause the minimum interference to those parts of the
reservoir area, but even so a small area was submerged.
Recognising the importance of scientific research in Upper
Teesdale, ICI Ltd contributed £100,000 for study during the ten-
year period 1967–1977.

The Dam stands 900 ft/274 m upstream of Cauldron Snout, and a
new footbridge had to be built to accommodate the Pennine Way,
as the original was submerged.

Cross over the fall by the new bridge, and follow the cart track
westwards to remote Birkdale Farm, a distance of 5 miles/8 km
from Langdon Beck, 143 miles/230 km from Edale.

Beyond Birkdale a path makes for the deserted mine cottage of
Moss Shop high up on the hillside, and from there crosses 2 miles/
3.2 km of open moor indistinctly, though cairned, among the
heather, bent and bog. The hollows in the ground hereabouts are
old craters, left by artillery fire from the ranges of Warcop, which
occupy the fells on the south side of Maize Beck.

Maize Beck is reached and crossed half a mile/0.8 km further on
near a sheepfold, though the stream is impossible to cross at this
point when the water is high. If the Beck is in flood keep to the
north bank for a further mile/1.6 km until a footbridge is reached
spanning a striking gorge, and return to the main path at High Cup

Remote Birkdale Farm on the route from Teesdale to the Vale of Eden

Nick. At the Maize Beck crossing by the main path strike across the shoulder of Murton Fell, leaving Maize Beck where it swings northwards, and soon you see the blue serrated outline of the Lakeland fells far away to the west. The path descends slightly then, suddenly, the land falls away at your very feet, and you are standing on the brink of the spectacular and colossal hollow of High Cup Nick.

Shaped like a horse-shoe, the whole of the rim is lined with a series of basaltic columns consisting of small buttresses and gullies. The land falls away sheer and the steep sides below are strewn with black scree. Beyond, the gill broadens into a lovely green plain and the Vale of Eden. High Cup Nick bears all the evidence of erosion by a valley glacier, and it may also have acted as an overflow channel for the Maize Beck lake. The stream that falls gently over the top is certainly too small to account for the extent to which the Nick has been cut.

The summit north of the Nick is Narrowgate Beacon, a name which recalls the days when beacon fires were lit on some of the Pennine tops to give warning of invasion threats and call the countrymen to arms.

A well-defined path leads to the north of the Nick and creeps round the edge of the precipice, and as you advance your attention is divided between the marvels of the cliff and patterned valley far below, and the beauty of the Lakeland panorama.

The path follows the edge of the Nick for over a mile/1.8 km at a fairly constant level, and when the rock buttresses merge with the slopes of the moor, follow a line of cairns which bear away to the right and guide you to a deserted quarry. Upon reaching a ruined limekiln near to a sheepfold, pass through a gate to a grassy track which crosses the slopes of Peeping Hill and gradually descends in a couple of miles/3.2 km to Dufton (7 miles/11.2 km from Birkdale; a total of 150 miles/241 km). Shapely, conical Dufton Pike and Knock Pike are disclosed as you pass through gated pastures down to the road in the village.

Dufton, with its red sandstone and colour-washed houses, is a pleasant village. The cottages are pleasantly arranged round an oblong green which is cut diagonally by the road and ornamented by

High Cup Nick

a well-executed stone fountain. Above the houses can be seen the flat top of Cross Fell, 6 miles/9.2 km away to the north.

Bed and breakfast accommodation may be available at the village Post Office or some of the cottages in Dufton. After a long absence a youth hostel was re-established in the village, and the one at Knock was closed. The welcome return of a hostel to Dufton saves an unwelcome detour after a long walk over and across the Pennine watershed.

Cross Fell from the Village Green at Dufton

Dufton to Cross Fell 9 miles/14.4 km

Where the road forks just outside Dufton a narrow track, becoming a footpath, leads northwards between Knock Pike and Dufton Pike to the Great Rundale Beck, then an old mine track leads us to Swindale Beck. The route then follows the stream bed up on to Green Fell and the summit of Knock Fell, 2,604 ft/794 m.

In 1952 the Nature Conservancy Council acquired 10,000 acres/ 4 047 ha of Knock Fell, Milburn Forest and Dufton Fell for the Moor House National Nature Reserve. This magnificent site high in the Pennines is an open-air laboratory for the investigation of the many problems of the ecology of the British moorlands.

From Knock Fell the route leads north-east of Green Castle, passing excavations and spoil heaps on the approach to Great Dun Fell and its radio station at 2,780 ft/847 m. Following an eight-day public inquiry in Penrith in July–August 1984 the Secretary of State for the Environment granted planning permission in November 1984 for the construction of a new long-range radar station on the top of Great Dun Fell and for the redevelopment of the existing air-ground-air radio station. The original buildings were erected in the 1940s and the new station was erected alongside. The new station is H-shaped with a central white radome 66 ft/20 m in diameter, glistening like a huge golfball. Originally designed to have two new masts 141 ft/43 m high, it was subsequently assessed that they wouldn't stand up to the strong winds, so the existing heavy timber lattice masts 60 ft/18.3 m high remain.

Work commenced in May 1985 and was completed by autumn 1986, and the station became operational in the spring of 1988. The station is the final link in a chain of new long-range radar stations extending from southern England to the Isle of Tiree, and cost £9.63 m to build.

Because of the severity of winter weather, no construction could take place between November and March, and the radar equipment has had to be covered by the dome to protect it from 150-knot winds—winds of 116 knots have already been experienced on Great Dun Fell—and temperatures of −20°c.

Cross Fell (left) and Great Dun Fell, taken from Knock Fell

Little Dun Fell

Great Dun Fell

Cross Fell

Cross Fell from Great Dun Fell

Little Dun Fell, 2761 ft/842 m, follows next, then you come to the boggy source of the River Tees, 8 miles/12.8 km from Dufton and 158 miles/254 km from Edale.

Climb north-westerly from Tees Head to the summit of Cross Fell, 2,930 ft/893 m, the highest point in the whole Pennine range. From the top are magnificent views over the Eden valley to the mountains of Lakeland, while to the north may be seen the silver ribbon of Solway, and beyond, Criffel and the hills of Galloway. Cross Fell was originally named 'Fiends' Fell'. According to tradition, St Augustine erected a cross on its summit, and, thus scattering the devils frequenting it, christened it Cross Fell.

Cross Fell is most often shrouded in low cloud and bad weather, and is the source of the Helm Wind. According to the glossary published by the Meteorological Office of the Air Ministry, the Helm Wind is a 'violent, cold, easterly wind blowing down the western slope of the Cross Fell range, Cumbria. It may occur at all seasons of the year, but mostly when the general direction of the wind is east or north-east. When the Helm is blowing a heavy bank of cloud (the Helm Cloud) rests along the range, and at a distance of 3 or 4 miles/4.8 to 6.4 km from the foot of the Fell— approximately along the line of the River Eden—a slender, nearly stationary roll of whirling cloud (the Helm Bar) appears in mid-air and parallel with the Helm Cloud. The cold wind blows strongly down the steep fell sides until it comes nearly under the Bar, when it suddenly ceases. To the west of this calm at the surface, a westerly wind may be experienced for a short distance. The space between the Helm Cloud and the Bar is usually quite clear, although the rest of the sky may be cloudy.'

The Helm is a powerful local wind, caused by cold air pouring down the steep scarp slope into the Eden Valley. The air becomes warmer as it descends, so that whirlpools of rising air are created, and these, rising and condensing, create the Helm Bar. The Helm Wind always stops short of the River Eden, and the contrasts, within a few yards, of its blowing and not blowing are very remarkable. The wind has been known to strip off heavy roofing slates and even uproot turnips from the fields, whilst on the opposite bank of the river one could hold a lighted match without its being blown out.

Cross Fell to Garrigill 7 miles/11.2 km

From the summit of Cross Fell descend by the easy north-west slopes to Cross Fell Well, joining the old corpse road at the western end of the Screes. Should you descend Cross Fell too much to the north your descent will be over rough and tumbled scree. If descending at the east end by traversing the top from the trig point, beware of a dangerous open mine shaft almost in your tracks—not far from Fallow Hill, 2,583 ft/787 m, and a boundary fence.

Follow the old corpse track on its easterly course to Garrigill. This track crosses the fells from Garrigill in South Tynedale to Kirkland in Eden. Coffin bearers no longer used this trail when ground was consecrated in Garrigill, but only after corpses had lain for weeks on the moor in a bad winter.

> Across the waste in bygone days,
> O'er lonely hills and marshy ways,
> There ran a road nor'-west;
> Between rough stones on either hand
> They carried through the dreary land
> The dead men to their rest.

This stony track crosses Skirwith Fell and passes some old mine workings, where one building has been made into a bothy, Greg's Hut, a suitable place for shelter, but not too comfortable to sleep in because of its stone flag floors. The track then leads over Alston Moor, crossing Pikeman Hill, 2,022 ft/616 m, Black Band Hill, 1,853 ft/565 m, then steeply down to Garrigill.

This track across Alston Moor is purple with Blue John crystals, the amethystine or topazine fluorspar generally believed to exist only at Castleton in Derbyshire. The moor is rich in ores—zinc blende, barytes, fluospar and galena, the most important of lead ores.

The Romans discovered lead in the neighbouring fells, destroying the forest trees for smelting. In the twelfth century silver and lead were the main attractions, and the Carlisle Lead Mines, as they were called, were granted the right to cut as much timber as they desired for smelting purposes.

Up to the time of the 1715 Jacobite Rising, the Alston area was

Cross Fell to Alston

Greg's Hut, the bothy on Cross Fell

owned by the Earls of Derwentwater, but after the participation of
the last Earl in the Stuart cause his lands were confiscated by the
Crown and were later granted to Greenwich Hospital. The
Commissioners have remained in possession ever since, and they
still draw revenue from the mining activities, as well as from the
rents of the hill farms. (Of the Earls of Derwentwater, James was
beheaded on Tower Hill on 24 February 1716, and his brother
Charles on 8 December 1746, for their activities in the Jacobite
Rebellion.)

In 1750 Greenwich Hospital leased the mines to the London Lead
Company, who worked most of the mines on Alston Moor until
1905, when the company was wound up. The Company played a
part in Tynedale and Teesdale that affected the whole life of the
valleys. Not only had the lead to be found, mined, smelted and
carried away, but the men who did the work had to be housed and
provided with at least the necessities of communal life.

Garrigill to Alston 4 miles/6.4 km

Garrigill is a small village at the head of the River South Tyne, lying
deep among the dark moors. Garrigill, 7 miles/11.2 km from Cross
Fell summit and 165 miles/265 km from Edale, is 15 miles/24 km
from the youth hostel at Dufton, and although meals and
accommodation may be obtained from the George and Dragon
Hotel by the village square, a greater choice of accommodation,
including a youth hostel, is at Alston, 4 miles/6.4 km down the
valley. The church displays a notice offering shelter, which if
accepted should not be abused.

From Garrigill the Pennine Way route continues downstream on
the left bank of the River South Tyne. After 2 miles/3.2 km at the
crossing of the Little Dry Burn cross the river by a footbridge to
Sillyhall, and from here follow the footpath through riverside
pastures to the road bridge at Alston, 169 miles/272 km from Edale.

As at Dufton, a youth hostel was re-established at Alston after a
long absence. With the blessing of Cumbria County Council and the
Countryside Commission a new purpose-built hostel was opened on
the line of the Pennine Way, built under the same National Parks

Act provisions as those at Crowden and Hawes. The next hostel is at Greenhead near Haltwhistle—9 miles/14.4 km from Alston and 7 miles/11.2 km from Once Brewed.

Garrigill in the South Tyne valley

Alston and the Maiden Way to Lambley 10 miles/16 km
Alston is a stone built town, the highest market town in England
and a good place for accommodation and supplies. The market
cross was erected by Sir William Stephenson, a native of the district
who was Lord Mayor of London in 1764.

At Alston cross the South Tyne bridge and continue downstream
on a path to Harbut Lodge and the Brampton road, B6292. Follow
this road north for 100 yds/91 m, then west to height 1,077 ft/328 m
and north-west to the Gilderdale Burn. This section of the route
around Harbut Lodge is difficult to follow, and from Alston it may
be easier to go by way of Raise, Nether Park and Park Fell to the
Maiden Way, following this Roman road northwards to the official
route at the Gilderdale Burn crossing.

The Maiden Way is one of the branches of the Ermine Street
system, connecting the camps at Kirkby Thore in the Eden valley
(which had direct connections with the camps and forts on the west
side of the Pennines), with the cross-country road at Stanegate and
Hadrian's Wall.

Follow the Maiden Way north again by Whitley Castle and beside
a stone wall to the Brampton road at Castle Nook. Whitley Castle
Roman Fort measures 150 × 128 yds/137 × 117 m and encloses 9
acres/3.6 ha, and stands on the open hillside commanding a
comprehensive view of the South Tyne valley. On three sides there
are four ramparts, but on the west, where the fort is overlooked by
a ridge of high ground, there are seven ramparts.

From Castle Nook cross the main road and continue on a path,
the line of the Maiden Way, through field gates to Kirkhaugh,
passing the church which is situated on the opposite bank of the
turbulent Tyne. The church has a tall needle-thin spire, and was
designed by its vicar without help from an architect, and modelled
upon one in the Black Forest in Germany.

The path continues between the road and railway line to Lintley,
where it crosses the railway, then rejoins the road again near
Slaggyford, 6 miles/9.6 km from Alston, 175 miles/282 km from

Alston, Cumbria, the highest market town in England

ston to Lambley

Edale. A road leaves the main village street on the left, and here a track leads right parallel to the railway to the Knar Burn, crosses under the railway, then by footpath to Merry Knowe and Burnstones by the Thinhope Burn. Knarsdale lies down the lane to the right, and in the churchyard is the curious epitaph of one Robert Baxter, who died on 4 October 1796:

> All you that please these lines to read,
> It will cause a tender heart to bleed;
> I murdered was upon the fell,
> And by the man I knew full well;
> By bread and butter which he'd laid,
> I, being harmless, was betrayed.
> I hope he will rewarded be,
> That laid that poison there for me.

Pass under the railway arch at Burnstones and bear right of the farm through fields to the line of the Roman road again, keeping the stone wall on your right till you reach the pretty Glendue Burn. Cross the burn by the footbridge and continue on the heather track of the Maiden Way. On the summit of the hill by a wire fence cross over a stile, which, although it means walking in heather, avoids several old fixed gates and very wet patches on the other side of the fence. At the Pennine Way sign, recross the fence and follow a grassy track down to the B6292, 4 miles/6.4 km from Slaggyford.

Lambley to Greenhead 7 miles/11.2 km
The route of the Pennine Way over Hartley Burn Common between Lambley and Greenhead is a complex and not very rewarding diversion that absorbs a great deal of time and energy. Although it is doubtful if many people would be willing to tramp the metalled road, it is recommended that following the line of the Maiden Way would be a suitable alternative and timesaver. This would avoid the wall and fence-infested official route, afford continuous and excellent views of South Tynedale, and give some sense of purpose by heading along the old Roman road striking directly at Carvoran and Hadrian's Wall. If opencast coal workings in the Lambley-Greenhead

area ever take place, as was predicted in the mid-1980s, the Pennine Way will then have to be diverted temporarily. As the Northumberland County Council have purchased from British Rail part of the old railway line between Haltwhistle and Lambley with the intention of making a footpath along it, there may be the opportunity of providing an alternative route down the South Tyne valley.

Cross the B6292 near Lambley and keeping a stone wall on your left pass by old colliery spoil heaps and two barns ahead which lead us to the Black Burn crossing, then cross the field north-westerly towards a prominent two-storey barn and down to the Hartley Burn. The route now runs upstream for about 300 yds/275 m then strikes north to reach a fence, which is followed on the right hand to join a path leading to Batey Shield and on to the Kellah Burn, where we leave the road at Greenriggs to cross Hartleyburn Common, past a ruined farmhouse on Wain Rigg and height 954 ft/ 289 m on Thirlwall Common.

To the north lie the lonely moors and forests of Spadeadam. Here in the early 1970s static firing tests were carried out on the engines of Blue Streak, Britain's first-stage rocket contribution to the joint European programme to launch a satellite into space. Today the site is largely empty, although the Ministry of Defence still occupy and maintain it. Part of the area was occupied by the British Gas Corporation for testing oil pipes to destruction, as part of the research into the technology of North Sea oil and gas exploitation. Spadeadam is now an electric bomb-testing range, and low-flying aircraft are everywhere.

A quarter of a mile/0.4 km south of the Hexham-Carlisle road A69 at Gap Shield Farm the Pennine Way turns east on a grassy track by Todholes barn and Tilesheds, then north-west and north to a village hall beside the main road half a mile/0.8 km west of Greenhead. Cross the A69 and pass through a wicket gate then north-easterly across a golf course over height 632 ft/193 m, dropping down to the golf club house near the Roman road of Stanegate. Follow Stanegate east to the Greenhead–Gilsland road, the railway line and the Tipalt Burn, 7 miles/11.2 km from Lambley, a total distance of 186 miles/300 km. Here we enter the Northumberland National Park.

Thirlwall Castle

We have now reached the line of Hadrian's Wall, though only the bare outlines of the Wall and its milecastles now remain. Here the Wall passed over a comparatively level tract of land, and was consequently more exposed to the attacks of the enemy. Aware of this, the Romans erected a thick line of defence a little to the south of the Wall, consisting of five camps placed about half a mile/0.8 km apart.

Many of the farmhouses and outbuildings have Roman stones built into the walls, while Thirlwall Castle by the Tipalt Burn was built entirely of Roman masonry. The castle is well seen from the footbridge as we cross the Tipalt Burn, a tall grey ruin of a tower with walls 9 ft/2.75 m thick. The youth hostel at Greenhead, converted from a hundred-year-old Primitive Methodist chapel, in the middle of the recently by-passed village, may be easily reached by a footpath running between the railway and the Burn south of the castle. The Greenhead Hotel in the village, or the Holmhead Guest House & Café on the Pennine Way by Thirlwall Castle, also provide accommodation.

From the Burn the ditch and vallum of the Roman Wall rise steeply to the site of Carvoran fort, and the start of our journey along Hadrian's Wall.

The Roman Wall, or Hadrian's Wall, was built about AD 125, and is the largest and probably best known monument of Roman antiquity in Britain. In AD 122 the Emperor Hadrian came to Britain and decided to build a barrier from the Tyne to the Solway to contain the northern tribes, as military panic had shattered the dream of a completely conquered Britain. The work of building the Wall was entrusted to the Legate of Britain, Aulus Platorius Nepos, and within ten years it was complete.

The garrison of the Wall was withdrawn shortly before AD 200 because of civil war on the Continent. The barbarians broke down the barriers, but the Wall was restored by the Emperor Septimus Severus. Then, in AD 383, Magnus Maximus led the British army on to the Continent against Gratian, and the Wall was finally abandoned after 250 years of usefulness.

The Wall extends for $73\frac{1}{2}$ English miles/118 km, or 80 Roman miles, from Wallsend-on-Tyne to Bowness-on-Solway. Though seldom above 6 ft/1.8 m high, even in the best preserved parts, it was once over 15 ft/4.5 m high, the parapet of the rampart wall bringing the total height to 20 ft/6 m. Though 9 ft 6 in/2.9 m thick in places, the average width is 7ft 6 in/2.2 m, the original and more generous plan being changed while the Wall was under construction.

The Wall

The interior of the Wall consisted of rubble and mortar, and the facing stones were quarried as close behind the Wall as possible. These stones, no larger than a man could carry, are 6–7 inches/15–17 cm high and 10–11 inches/25–28 cm wide, and sometimes extend as much as 20 inches/50 cm into the Wall, tapering inwards in order to bond better. In all, the Wall contained over two million cubic yards/1.5 million cubic metres of material! The Wall was built by the legionaries themselves. Each century acted as an independent working party, building a length of about 50 yds/45 m and then moving on to a similar length elsewhere, thus the joints between the sections did not always conform.

The Forts

On the Wall were 17 forts, 3–7 miles/4.8–11.2 km apart. The larger
forts, of about 5 acres/2 ha, accommodated 1,000 infantry or 500
cavalry, while the smaller forts, of 3 acres/1.2 ha held 500 infantry.
The forts generally projected beyond the Wall, but on cliff edges
were parallel with it. The walls of the forts were 5 ft/1.5 m thick, and
were reinforced by an internal earth bank derived from a defensive
ditch running round the outside. The internal stone buildings
included barracks, a colonnaded headquarters building, the
commandant's house, and workshops. There were also granaries to
hold the year's corn supply received as tribute from the tribes
protected by the Wall. Outside each fort was a spacious suite of
baths, various temples and shrines, and a village for the soldiers'
wives and other civilians.

The Milecastles

More regularly spaced were the milecastles, which were normally
separated by a distance of 1,620 yds/1 481 m, a Roman mile. These
were roughly 20 yds/18 m square and held perhaps fifty men as
patrols for sentry duty. Between each pair of milecastles, about 540
yds/493 m apart, were two turrets, measuring 14 ft/4.26 m square
and holding four men.

   The patrolling garrison in the milecastles and turrets must have
consisted of some 5,000 auxiliary troops, while the more highly
trained fighting garrison stationed at the forts numbered about
14,000.

The Ditch

The Wall was protected on its northern side by a V-shaped ditch 27
ft/8 m wide and 9 ft/2.75 m deep. The excavated material was laid to
form a broad mound to heighten the ditch and laid on the south side
so as to form no cover for the enemy. The ditch is always present
except where the Wall stands on the edge of a cliff, and can be
followed for miles even in places where the Wall itself has
disappeared.

The Vallum

Running roughly parallel with the Wall on its south side is a much

more impressive ditch called the Vallum. It is normally 60–80 yds/
54.8–73 m south of the Wall, but runs straight for long distances, to
give it a total length of some 60 miles/96.5 km.

The Vallum consists of a ditch 10 ft/3 m deep, 20 ft/6 m wide at
the top and 8 ft/2.4 m across the flat bottom. Thirty feet/9 m away
on each side of the ditch, and parallel with it, lies a mound 20 ft/6 m
wide, formed of the material dug from the ditch. The whole work of
the Vallum is thus 120 ft/56.5 m across, and must have taken a
million man-days to dig.

The Vallum was the southern boundary of the patrolled military
zone along the Wall, and at the same time a customs barrier to
civilians. Public entry to the military zone was by unfortified gates
controlled from the forts, there being no other access to the Wall at
other points.

The Military Way
A Military Way connects the forts, milecastles and turrets, and runs
between the Wall and the Vallum. It was a metalled road about 20
ft/6 m wide, and its course can be followed because all the field-
gates are placed upon it. Troops could be secretly moved along this
road to issue forth at the milecastles or forts in unexpected sallies
against the enemy.

The Stanegate
Another Roman road called the Stanegate runs a mile or so south of
the Vallum, and connected the main trunk roads to the north. It was
built by Julius Agricola, Governor of Britain from about AD 75 to
85, and was used as the main military base-line for Hadrian's new
frontier till the decision was reached to move more troops up to the
Wall itself.

After the withdrawal of the legions the Military Way and the
Stanegate became neglected, and Newcastle was connected with
Carlisle by nothing more than a muddy track. In 1745 General
Wade's army took three days to cover the 22 miles/35.4 km from
Newcastle to Hexham, and Carlisle thus fell into the hands of Prince
Charles. As a result a new West Turnpike was constructed in

1751–3, the line between Newcastle and Chollerford being the direct route taken by Hadrian's Wall. The landowners were pleased to sell the useless stone-covered ground beside the Wall, and the fallen material formed a firm foundation.

Along the actual course of the Wall we are often too concerned with features of antiquarian interest to pay attention to the scenery. The Whin Sill ridge which Hadrian's Wall follows for a greater part of its length forms precipitous crags which face northwards across a wild and barren country. The great ice sheet came up against this hard basalt escarpment, to gouge out the softer rocks at the base and leave its aftermath in a series of boggy mosses and basins occupied by lakes or loughs. These loughs, though not very large, gain in impressive dignity by their proximity to the towering dark crags surmounted by the reminders of a long-past military power and discipline.

What is left of the Wall is glorious testimony to the might of ancient Rome. How glorious it is, how great a spell it casts, is known only to those who have wandered along some of its lonely miles in the hills, and with no sound save the wind singing in their ears or a curlew crying in the sedge. No sight in all England is more impressive than the Roman Wall, this thick grey line rolling up hill and down dale as it has done through the centuries, since the days when Christianity itself was young.

The 9-mile/14.4 km length of the Roman Wall is quite clear to
follow though the markings on the older Ordnance Survey maps are
confusing, and the Map of Hadrian's Wall at a scale of 1:31,680 may
be more useful.

Carvoran Fort
The fort of Carvoran covers an area of 3½ acres/1.4 ha, but
unhappily it has largely been destroyed by agricultural operations
and all that is left above the surface are a few ploughed-up stones
and the remains of the north-west tower. Some fragments of the
northern rampart remain, and these must have been the ruins which
William Camden found 'very evident' in 1599.

Carvoran is situated on high ground to the south of both Vallum
and Wall and was probably erected before them, guarding the
junction of the Stanegate with the Maiden Way which comes up to
the south-east angle of the station.

The most remarkable discovery of all at Carvoran was made in
1915, just outside the north-east angle of the fort. A postman
delivering letters to the neighbouring farmhouse saw what looked
like an old bucket projecting from the boggy ground. On picking it
up he found that it was a well-made Roman dry measure in bronze,
in perfect condition. The measure bears an inscription saying that it
holds 17½ sextarii (16.8 pints/10 litres). Roman certified measures
are normally quite accurate, though this measure really holds nearly
20 pints/11 litres, and it is thought that the inscription was a means
of cheating the natives when they brought their tribute of corn. The
bronze measure is the most remarkable single object exhibited in
Chesters Museum.

Carvoran to Walltown Milecastle
Beyond Carvoran cross the Walltown Quarry road, taking the lane
that runs south of the quarry to Walltown Wood. Immediately after
passing through the first cattle grid on this lane, turn north to where
the Wall resumes the basaltic range of the Whin Sill along the Nine
Nicks of Thirlwall. The Nine Nicks are so named from that number

of peaks in the rocky ridge, though the first four nicks have been removed by quarry operations.

A fine stretch of Wall runs to Turret 45a, a prominent long-distance signal tower now in ruins. From here views extend from Cross Fell and Skiddaw in the south, the broad flash of Solway in the west, while to the north stretches the moorland waste to which the eye has become accustomed for many miles.

To the east runs the mighty basaltic ridge. The Wall traverses this to the top of Walltown Crags and Milecastle 45 (Walltown) on the top, then descends the steep west side of Walltown Nick. Walltown Nick is a wide one, and here the ditch reappears to strengthen the gap. Close behind the Wall, in the middle of the gap, is a spring surrounded by masonry called 'King Arthur's Well'. According to tradition this is where Paulinus baptised King Egbert. In the crevices of the whinstone rock hereabouts grow abundant patches of chives, said to have been planted by the Romans.

Walltown to Alloa Lea

Overlooking Walltown Nick is Turret 44b, and then follows Mucklebank Crag at 860 ft/262 m the highest peak in the ridge of the Nine Nicks of Thirlwall. Beyond the eighth nick comes Turrett 44a at the turn on the crest, and the Wall descends into the ninth and final nick.

The Military Way at this point is very plain to see, and we soon come to the grassy foundations and rounded southern corners of Milecastle 44 (Alloa Lea) half hidden by the bracken of Haltwhistle Common. From Alloa Lea Milecastle the Wall descends gradually to Cockmount Hill Wood—a fine stretch exhibiting six, seven and even nine courses of stones in its north face. The ditch is very irregular, dug sometimes fully, sometimes to half-width, and often not at all. At the west end of Cockmount Hill Wood is a circular milestone from the Military Way forming a gatepost on the line of the Wall.

Great Chesters Fort

To the east we next come to Aesica or Great Chesters Fort, smaller than either Chesters or Housesteads, but except for the specialist in Roman history it hardly repays a visit. Aesica measures 140 × 120 yds/128 × 109 m, and part of the 3 acre/1.2 ha site is now occupied by farm buildings. The ramparts are still clearly defined, the west wall being well preserved to a height of about 5 ft/1.5 m. There are traces of watch towers at the north-west and south-west corners. In the centre of the fort is a dilapidated vaulted chamber filled with ferns—the underground strongroom which lay beneath the Shrine of the Standards.

Excavations in 1939 indicated that Aesica was built during the construction of the Wall; and also that it was an afterthought, for a newly built milecastle (No. 43) had to be demolished to accommodate it. Just outside the east gate was discovered an inscription describing Hadrian as the father of his country; this proved the fort to be not earlier than AD 128, when this title was bestowed on Hadrian.

The water supply to the fort was obtained from the head of Caw Burn, 2¼ miles/3.6 km away, by means of an aqueduct, now choked, 3–4 ft/0.9–1.2 m deep and about as wide, which winds for a distance of about 6 miles/9.6 km to avoid bridges or embankments.

Visitors to the Black Gate Museum at Newcastle can see the famous collection of jewellery found in the south gate of Aesica in 1894. There is a silver chain collar with a pendant, a silver bangle, a gold ring, a bronze ring set with a gem, and a huge silver brooch. Above all, there is the famous Aesica Brooch of gold, a masterpiece of Celtic art, made about the year 100.

From Aesica the Wall bends eastwards at Turret 42b. From here the ditch is boldly developed, but the Wall is for the most part traceable only by the ruins on its foundations. Just before Burnhead Farm pass through a gate to the north side of the Wall and to the crossing at the Haltwhistle Burn.

Just below this crossing a large Roman watermill was excavated in 1908. Part of the undershot wooden mill-wheel was found, and the big mill-stones are exhibited in Chesters Museum. The mill is now buried by quarry spoil, and Turret 42a nearby has been destroyed by quarrying.

Haltwhistle Burn Camps

Around this area are a remarkable group of temporary camps, thought to have sheltered men building the Wall. A little to the south of the Wall where the Carlisle road crosses the Haltwhistle Burn can be seen the deep grass-covered ditches of Haltwhistle Burn Fort. The fort appears to have been added to the Stanegate early in Hadrian's reign to guard the stream crossing. This was at a time when it had been decided to build the Wall, but while it was still intended to keep the main military concentration on the Stanegate. When the Wall was built the fort was demolished, and was partly buried beneath the refuse of a Roman quarry.

Two miles to the south lies Haltwhistle, a quiet little industrial town pleasantly situated amid beautiful scenery near the River South Tyne. Bed and breakfast accommodation is available at the Red Lion and Manor House hotels, but if lodging has been found near Greenhead it will not be too far to continue eastwards along the Wall to the youth hostel at Once Brewed.

Cawfields

Back to the line of the Wall again follow the track at the foot of the quarry to Hole Gap, where the Wall follows Cawfields Crags. The old quarry has been made into a picnic site with car park and toilets. The tarmacadam track is the official route, leading towards Cawfields Farm, but the path beside the quarry pond is more attractive. Leave the quarry foot and climb a track to a gate in the fence, turning left to the renovated Milecastle 42 (Cawfields). The milecastle measures internally 63 × 49 ft/19.2 × 14.9 m, and its 8 ft/2.4 m thick walls are 7 to 8 courses of masonry high. The gateways, both on the northern and southern sides, are of large dimensions, and the pivot holes may still be seen. It is difficult to speculate why this milecastle should differ from the rest in having a gateway to the north, as it opens directly on to the edge of the crag, which is precipitous.

Opposite Cawfields Milecastle the Vallum is in a state of preservation hardly equalled in any other part of its course, where it runs uninterrupted in a straight line for almost 5 miles/8 km. The planning of the Military Way is also interesting. It crosses the north

mound of the Vallum, travels for 250 yds/228 m along the north
berm, and then recrosses the mound. The position of the Vallum
left no room for the road, although had the road been contemplated
when the Vallum was laid out, nothing would have been easier than
to place the Vallum a little more to the south. The road is thus later
in the frontier scheme than either Wall or Vallum.

Cawfields Crags to Winshields Crags

The Wall is in an excellent state over Cawfields Crags to Turret 41b,
but afterwards is for some distance nearly uprooted. Pass Thorny
Doors and Bloody Gap, then the site of Turret 41a, gently dropping
down into Caw Gap. Opposite the turret the ditch reappears,
though only for a few yards. A road passes through Caw Gap,
where the Wall, as usual, bends to the south on either side, so as to
protect the line of attack. To the north of the gap is a lonely
farmhouse called Burn Deviot, formerly the resort of smugglers and
sheep-stealers, and now inhabited, it is alleged, by the spirits of the
persons murdered there. Two large stones to the south of the gap
near the Carlisle road are called the Mare and Foal, and are
probably the remains of a Druid circle.

   The next broad depression is Boggle Hole Gap, and a gentle
ascent brings us to Milecastle 41 (Melkridge), 1,641 yds/1 500 m
east of Cawfields Milecastle. Next comes the ridge itself and Turret
40b, and the deep valley of Lowdham Slacks, where the Wall
acquires its ditch again.

   The Wall then ascends Winshields Crags, attaining an elevation
of 1,230 ft/345 m, the highest point throughout its course. A wide
and magnificent view extends from Scotland to Cross Fell. Here a
fine piece of the Wall is preserved by English Heritage. An 8 ft/
2.4 m wall stands on a foundation 10 ft/3 m wide: the foundations
had already been laid when a change of plan reduced the width,
though the north face remains unbroken.

Winshields Crags to Peel Crags

The Wall descends the basalt ridge and passes the remains of
Milecastle 40 (Winshields), which has walls uniformly 6 ft 9 in/2 m
thick. The distances between this milecastle and milecastles 41 and

39 are exceptionally long, measuring 1,850 and 1,806 yds/1 691 and 1 651 m respectively, when the usual measurement was as close to 1,620 yds/1 481 m as possible.

Beyond Winshields Milecastle the ditch begins again, and continues as far as the gap at Steel Rigg. Steel Rigg is a good spot from which to leave the Wall if accommodation for the night is required—either at the inn of Twice Brewed or the youth hostel at Once Brewed, half a mile/0.8 km south on the Carlisle road.

The new inn of Twice Brewed replaces a famous coaching inn of the same name, and good meals may be obtained there on request. Further to the east and immediately south of Peel Gap at a crossroads is the Once Brewed Youth Hostel. The original hostel was acquired in 1934 and occupied former farm buildings, but accommodation was limited and a new hostel was built alongside. It was opened in Easter 1968. Alongside the youth hostel is an information centre with toilets and car park. The centre contains a display of material relating to the Northumberland National Park, including photographs, relief model and large-scale plan of the Hadrian's Wall area. It is 14 miles/22.5 km from Once Brewed to the next youth hostel at Bellingham.

Diversion to Chesterholme

Once Brewed is perhaps the best place to mention the camp at Chesterholme, the Roman Vindolanda, some 2 miles/3.2 km east down the course of the Brackie's Burn, and standing alongside the line of Agricola's original road, the Stanegate. The camp covers $3\frac{1}{2}$ acres/1.4 ha and is under the guardianship of English Heritage, and of particular interest is a Roman milestone, beside Brackie's Burn and Stanegate. Uninscribed and nearly 6 ft/1.8 m high, the milestone has the distinction of being the only one in Britain in its original position. A section of the Wall has been constructed in stone and in turf, to show its original height, and there is also an excellent museum.

Steel Rigg to Crag Lough

However, our interest lies mainly along the line of the Wall, and we return to the basalt ridge at Steel Rigg, where there is a car park and toilets. A fine stretch of Wall runs eastward from the road, and the section of Wall from Steel Rigg to Housesteads is under the care of the National Trust. Where the Wall descends a steep cliff into Peel Gap, an obviously weak point in the defence, the Wall bends to the south, then to the east, then to the north again, thus enclosing the valley on three sides.

The Wall runs steeply up the side and along the edge of Peel Crag where tall and precipitous basaltic columns cling to the side of the steep drop to tne north. Here the Wall is in fine condition, with Turret 39a in its south face. The cutting and embankment of the Military Way south of the turret are well worth viewing.

After Turret 39a is another depression known as Cat's Stairs, offering a precarious route to the bottom of the crag. Further east is another depression into Castle Nick where there are the remains of a well-preserved milecastle—Milecastle 39 (Peel).

Peel Milecastle measures some 50 ft/15 m from east to west and 62 ft/18.8 m from north to south. The side walls are 7 ft/2.1 m thick and have six or seven courses still standing. At the northwest corner are the remains of a small barrack building, and foundations of other apartments still remain. South of Castle Nick the Military Way appears in very perfect condition, with kerbstones complete on each side. Its course can be followed because the well-drained foundations permit finer grass to grow upon it than elsewhere.

The Wall rises steeply from Castle Nick and runs along the verge of the cliff, then sharply turns to the south and descends into Steel Rigg Gap, where the Wall stones are stepped horizontally into the face of the ground. Now the Wall clings to the very edge of the precipice of High Shields Crag and passes through a little copse, affording occasional pleasant views of Crag Lough and Hotbank Crags beyond.

The Wall descends into Milking Gap, and is again accompanied by the ditch, and then bends at a sharp angle to take the ascent of Hotbank Crags.

Crag Lough is a shallow little mere, darkened by the reflection of the black basalt cliffs rising 200 ft/60 m sheer from the water. The eastern end and northern shores are bounded by marshy ground with natural thickets of willow, and among the reeds moorhens,

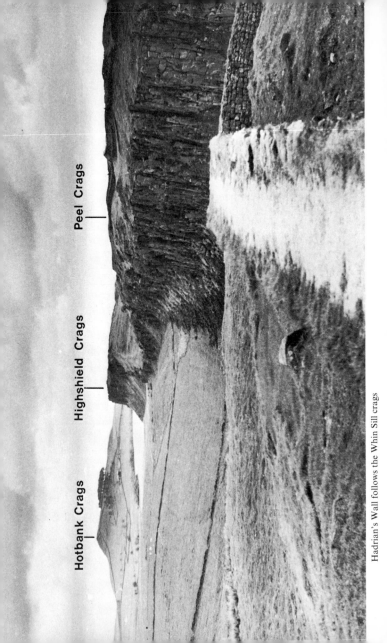

Hotbank Crags   Highshield Crags   Peel Crags

Hadrian's Wall follows the Whin Sill crags

Hotbank Crags

Highshield Crags

Crag Lough

Milecastle 39

Hadrian's Wall, looking east from Castle Nick

Hotbank Farm from Crag Lough

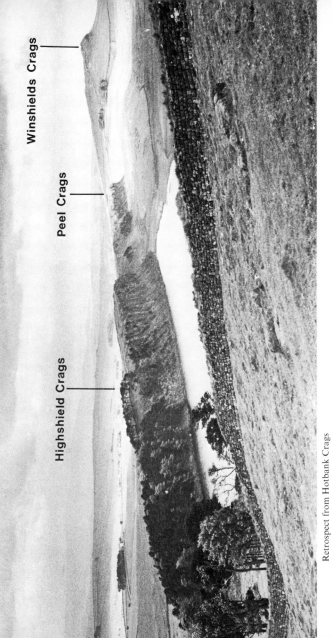

Winshields Crags

Peel Crags

Highshield Crags

Retrospect from Hotbank Crags

Sewingshields Crags

Housesteads Milecastle

Hadrian's Wall from Cuddy's Crags

swans and wild duck make their nests. Here may be found different species of pond weed, the yellow water lily, the reed mace and other botanical specimens. In the crevices of the crag rowans cling, and mountain parsley fern and saxifrage grow.

South of Milking Gap the broad shoulder of Barcombe Hill rises above Chesterholme camp, with a magnificent view from the Long Stone on its summit of the Roman Wall stretching from the Nine Nicks of Thirlwall to Sewingshields Crags.

Hotbank to Housesteads

In Milking Gap pass through a gateway in the Wall, and follow the course of the Wall on its south side as it ascends from Hotbank Farm. Opposite Hotbank Farm are the turf-covered remains of Milecastle 38 (Hotbank). This was partly excavated in 1935 and an inscribed stone was found, recalling its building by the Second Legion under Aulus Platorius Nepos, who was the Governor of Britain from AD 122 to 126.

The Wall climbs the hill to Hotbank Crags, with its fine views of the Northumberland lakes. The largest is the beautiful Greenlee Lough, north of the Crags. This is one of the places where the white water-lily grows wild, and in autumn and winter is the haunt of scores of swans. To the east stretches the lovely expanse of Broomlee Lough. Looking back the way we have come, Crag Lough and the mighty Whin Sill crags form a picture of impressive grandeur, the black crags rising thickly wooded above the sombre lake, and the sheer bare cliffs receding into the distance.

The Wall runs splendidly along the cliffs, and in many places is in excellent condition. This sector is cared for by the National Trust, which has built up the south face of the Wall, though the north face is still in disrepair, and the remains of Turrets 37a and 37b are buried. To the east the Wall disappears for a time and it is best to walk along the Military Way to the site of Turret 37a in the steep defile of Rapishaw Gap, a favourite pass for moss-troopers. A drovers' road leads northwards on to the wild moors beyond Greenlee Lough. This is the route of the Pennine Way on the next stage through Wark Forest to Bellingham, and we return to this point when we have visited Housesteads Fort.

Housesteads Milecastle

Housesteads Milecastle

From Rapishaw Gap the Wall ascends Cuddy's Crags, with the most celebrated view of the Wall surging up and down the rocky heights. The Wall dips then rises again to Milecastle 37 (Housesteads), the finest example of these structures now to be seen. The Milecastle is of a pattern closely resembling that at Cawfields, and was built by the same legion. It measures 50 × 60 ft/ 15 × 18 m, and the north wall stands 14 courses or 9 ft 6 in/2.89 m high. There are some excellent photographs of excavations made in 1933 exhibited in Housesteads Museum.

Housesteads Fort

Housesteads is the finest and best preserved of all the seventeen forts that housed the auxiliary regiments on Hadrian's Wall. The fort measures 610 × 367 ft/186 × 111 m, covers an area of 5 acres/ 2 ha, and is set in a fine commanding spot on the edge of the basalt cliff. The ruins are extensive and perfect, the bad reputation of the district due to the activities of moss-troopers saving the fort from destruction. These horse-stealers and plunderers raided the neighbouring countryside, and many pele-towers and fortified houses still exist to remain as evidence of their activities. It was not until the early 1700s that the last moss-troopers ceased to hold Housesteads as their den.

The entrance to the fort is through the south gateway, paying a small charge to the custodian for the privilege. This is also the main entrance used by visitors who have left their vehicles by the Carlisle road, and have climbed the hill to the fort past the remains of the civil settlement.

The South Gate

Entering Housesteads by the South Gate into the Via Praetoria, we are struck by the massive masonry remaining, the south wall standing ten or twelve courses high. The north and south gates are nearer to the east side of the fort than the west, so the main streets cut the fort into four unequal parts.

The guardchambers of the gateway are still there on both sides, but that on the east was occupied by some moss-troopers who added a tower outside the Wall and built a lime-kiln inside. The pivot-

A tour of Housesteads Fort

HOUSESTEADS ROMAN FORT
AFTER A SURVEY BY A.C. DICKIE AND R.C. BOSANQUET.

BUILDINGS 1 -VI BARRACKS

Housesteads Fort: The Latrines

holes for the gates are still visible, and so are the marks of chariot wheels on the flag stones. The Via Praetoria running north is not in its original state, and at some time a building was erected across it just inside the gateway.

The Latrines
Following the inside of the fort wall to the east, we come in the south-east corner to the latrines. This is an oblong building with a central paved walk bordered by channels, once excavated but now covered, around which runs a deep sewer that was once covered by seats for which a few dowel holes remain. There is a large stone trough inside the latrines which was probably used for washing clothes.

Near the latrines, behind the south-east angle tower, is the best preserved water tank in the fort, once fed by a spout from the flat roof of the tower. The large stone slabs which form its sides are jointed with lead, and bound together with iron straps set in lead. The inner face of the slabs accommodates iron hold-fasts set in lead, which held a vanished lead lining in position. Outlet holes at different levels fed a stone channel at ground level for flushing the latrine system. The top edges of the tank are much worn, having been used by the soldiers for sharpening their weapons.

The fort appears to have had no wells inside it, and evidently all the rainwater from the roofs of the buildings was collected and used. The gutters for leading water to various points have been discovered, and the whole drainage system illustrates the care devoted by the Roman army to matters of hygiene affecting the health of their troops.

The East Gate
Turn left up the hill to the East Gate, the main entrance to the fort from the Military Way. The eastern wall, which is 5 ft/1.5 m thick has been cleared of the earthen rampart which enabled the soldiers to man the defences, and the massive masonry can be closely examined.

The East Gate consists of two portals. The south portal was blocked up in the second century, while the threshold of the north portal still exhibits the holes in which the pivots moved, the stones against which the gates stuck when they were closed, and the 8 in/20 cm deep ruts caused by the chariot wheels. These grooves are 4 ft 8½ ins/143.5 cm apart, the modern British Railway gauge. The story, however, that this gauge was based upon them is without foundation. George Stephenson determined the dimension, some years before the gateway was discovered, on the instruction of Howard Pease, by averaging the measurements of 100 country carts. It is coincidence that the wheel gauge of Roman carts approximated to that found convenient ever since.

From this gateway to the opposite one in the west ran the main street, or Via Principalis. Immediately west of the East Gate are seen the remains of a long building of very solid masonry, furnished with a small set of baths at its east end. This appears to be a range set apart for social uses, as opposed to the normal barrack or stable block.

Proceeding northwards along the inside of the east wall we come to a converted interval tower, one of several to be seen around the walls. The tower has been strengthened by a solid platform of masonry for holding a catapult or ballista, and past this we continue to the North-East tower where the Wall joins the fort.

The North-East Tower

The North-East angle tower of the fort seems to have been moved after the Wall was built, an indication that the fort was built before the Wall. From here there is a good view of the Wall leading down to the Knag Burn and up to King's Hill and Sewingshields Crag.

The Knag Burn

Below in the dip lies the Knag Burn Gate where there was a customs barrier, a gateway facilitating trade with the civil settlement of the fort and the tribesmen to the north. The gateway was flanked by guardchambers and closed by door both at back and front, enabling a careful check to be made of those who were permitted to cross the frontier. Nearby the Knag Burn runs under the Wall in a remarkable culvert, still covered with slabs and paved at the bottom.

Housesteads Fort : The Granary

The North Gate

Follow the northern wall of the fort to the North Gate. The gateway appears to lead into space, but it had a roadway ramp leading up to it, though this was removed to reveal the interesting foundations to better advantage. The North Gate is beautifully built and still massive in ruins, the outside of the north rampart wall being one of the finest pieces of masonry on the line of the Wall.

From the North Gate to the centre of the fort we follow the Via Praetoria. On the east side of this street is a very large building, 147 ft/44.8 m long and 30 ft/9 m wide. At its eastern end are several small chambers, one of them having been heated by flues beneath the floor, and another containing a cistern or bath. On the west side of the street are two large apartments—one 78 ft/23.7 m long and 18 ft/5.4 m wide, the other not quite so long, having at its western end a moss-trooper's kiln for drying corn. Some of these large buildings were doubtless the halls in which the public business of the district was transacted, and others were used as the residence of the prefect and his chief officers. The foundation walls of many other chambers, inhabited chiefly by the ordinary soldiers, remain, but there is little to indicate the internal arrangements of them.

The Granaries

Just south of the North Gate are two great granaries, the southern one containing a moss-trooper's corn-drying kiln. The northern granary clearly exhibits ventilators in the walls and a forest of short stone pillars which supported the wooden floor joists. In the southern wall socket holes where the beams rested to support the floor are still visible. The purpose of this raised floor, with ventilation below it, was to keep the stored corn cool and dry, while the external buttresses reinforced the outer wall, cut by the ventilators, against the weight of piled wheat. Between the central walls of the granaries is a row of pillars, and it is thought that originally these supported the roof, but maybe after the original building was demolished it was found easier to divide the granary into two by means of the centre walls. The buildings were entered from the west, where the wide thresholds of their great double doors are to be seen.

Housesteads Fort: The West Gate

The Headquarters Building

A few yards below the granaries is the Principia, or Headquarters Building, at the junction of the Via Principalis and Via Praetoria. Little is left of the foundations, but sufficient to show the general plan. At the entrance were fine reliefs of Mars and Victory, and these are now in the Chesters Museum. The front courtyard had a verandah supported on columns, and was later walled off into rooms. The column bases can still be seen. From the courtyard an archway led into the Cross Hall. In this was the seat of justice, and the remains of the dais can be seen in the north-west corner. From this hall there were the usual five openings into the Shrine of the Standards and the Regimental Offices. In a room beside the Shrine were found over 800 arrow heads with traces of their wooden shafts still sticking to them. They are now on display at Chesters Museum.

The Commandant's House

The Commandant's House stood to the south of the Principia, but very little of it is left uncovered. Westwards are more barrack buildings and the remains of the hospital, but they have not been completely excavated.

The West Gate

We now come to the West Gate, the finest and most complete of all the gateways to the fort, eleven courses of masonry high. At some period following its erection the northern portal of the outside gate and the southern portal of the inside gate were blocked up, thus making the entrance passage a diagonal one. The threshold has been worn by the tread of feet, and many projecting stones in the outside wall have been rounded and hollowed by the soldiers sharpening their weapons upon them. The pivot holes for the doors are well seen, and also for the bar which fastens them. The locking device is an inverted 'L' shaped groove into which the bar was slid, the other end fitting into a hole in the opposite wall. The doors themselves were about 5 inches/12.7 cm thick.

Housesteads Museum

Outside the West Gate turn left down the hill towards the Museum, outside the southwest angle of the fort. The museum does not contain many of the treasures of Housesteads, these being at Chesters Museum and some at the Black Gate Museum in Newcastle. However, it contains a very good model of the fort as it was in Roman times, and models of the West Gate and one of the buildings in the civil settlement. There are detailed plans and photographs of some of the buildings and early excavation works.

Hadrian's Wall to Wark Forest 2 miles/3.2 km

Leaving Housesteads now we can return to the Pennine Way by
crossing the fields westwards along the line of the Military Way for
$\frac{1}{2}$-mile/0.8 km to Rapishaw Gap. Before passing through the
gateway we can take a look to the south, and catch a quick glimpse
of the rolling Pennine massif, high, bare, and uncompromising. The
landscape to the north to which we now turn is not so different to
that of Roman times, despite the skyline becoming marred by the
conifers of the Forestry Commission.

Over the wild and open moors the moss-troopers raided and
rustled each other's cattle and sheep. No more are these fells wild
and open, for the Forestry Commission have covered them with the
largest forests in Britain, stretching from the Roman Wall to the
Cheviots themselves, and this has swept all the sheep off the fells
and closed and left derelict numerous farmhouses. It was as though
the hills had been enveloped in a green cloud, where each fell top
has lost its individual character and streams have been spirited away
among the relentless smoothing tide of trees.

Not only do these vast plantations of the Forestry Commission
indicate a change of topography. On this, the Pictish side of the
Wall, the valleys lie in great concave basins between narrow ridges,
whence the eye ranges mile after mile over great stretches of
country to the next ridge that jags the skyline. On the southern side
of the Wall narrow valleys cleave great convex moorlands, so that
views are limited either to the tops of the moors or the narrow limits
of the valley.

The Pennine Way crosses the Wall and goes due north on an old
drove road to a ruined lime kiln, then continues over a piece of
somewhat boggy ground, crossing Jenkins Burn and passing
between Broomlee and Greenlee Loughs.

The moors to the north put the Roman Wall itself in a proper
perspective. Looking back, we can see that the few courses of stone
crowning the Whin Sill soon melt into the distant panorama of
moorland. Only the heights around remain—or did so until the

Housesteads to Bellingham

Forestry Commission got to work and began to change the untamed face of Northumberland.

The track passes the ruins of Crag End, and crosses over to a farm gate just past East Stonefolds Farm.

The track has been easy to follow and as it mounts the slopes beyond Stonefolds it is still well defined as it leads towards Haughtongreen. But here the forest zone is reached, and foresters, however well meaning they may be, seem to have a habit of upsetting even the best of tracks. Not that there is any lack of paths through the trees. Indeed, their very multiplicity is puzzling, so much so that it becomes difficult to separate fire-ride from authentic track.

A track leads northwards through the forest to emerge at Middleburn, but this is not the one we want: the track we need to follow emerges a little to the west of Ladyhill, and it is easy to follow provided that in the forest you follow the line of the telegraph wires.

Black Dike

From Stonefolds continue generally northwards on the forest road and after about 1 mile/1.6 km fork right on a path to emerge at a gate opening out on to Hawkside Fell. The eastern boundary of the forest follows the line of the Black Dike, an ancient cutting and earthwork of unknown antiquity, supposed to be the boundary line between the kingdoms of Northumbria and Cumbria. It can be traced in places from the North Tyne (at High Cariteth near Tarset) to the South Tyne (at Moralee between Haydon Bridge and Bardon Mill). It cannot be seen on boggy ground, but elsewhere may be noticed as a ditch 14 ft/4.2 m across and 4–6 ft/1.2–1.8 m deep; the excavated earth forms a mound on the east side, indicating that the area cut off was to the east of the Dike in the fork of the two Tynes.

Kimmin's Cross

The crossing of Haughton Common is not very easy going, but from 1,078 ft/329 m on Hawk Side bear east on a green track towards the foundations of Kimmin's Cross, on the south edge of the forest beside a gate bearing a fire warning sign. (The location of Kimmin's

Hawk Side

Retrospect from Kimmin's Cross

Cross is now correctly marked on the 1:50,000 scale maps, but is spelt Comyn's Cross; all now remaining is a pile of stones.) According to legend Kimmin (or Cumming or Comyn), a northern chieftain, was slain on this spot by the jealous sons of King Arthur after he had paid a visit to the King at his castle near Sewingshields.

From Kimmin's Cross we re-enter the forest, and descend by forest rides generally northwards through the plantations to emerge on a lane just west of Ladyhill, a distance of 6 miles/9.6 km from Housesteads, 201 miles/323 km from Edale. Opposite Ladyhill a Pennine Way sign points northwards, and a track leads north-easterly skirting the forest, crossing Fawlee Sike and leading to the Warks Burn.

Warks Burn to Bellingham 5 miles/8 km

Across the Warks Burn the route becomes easier to follow. A footpath leads past Horneystead to Ash and a track continues to the road, where turn to the right and then turn off left at Leadgate Cottage by a green track to Low Stead and Linacres by the Blacka Burn. From Low Stead turn east to the road, turn north to the road junction, where a footpath descends to the wild and rapid Houxty Burn and a footbridge to Shitlington Hall.

Shitlington Hall is written in old documents as Shotlyngton Hall, and this house superseded the old manor house of a branch of the Charlton family. In 1528 it was recorded that a band of Border thieves, led by 'Willie o' Shotlyngton' and others, raided neighbouring Wolsingham, robbing many houses and carrying off the priest of Muggleswick as prisoner. William Charlton was killed in the pursuit which followed, and his body afterwards hung in chains in Hexham.

Keep Shitlington Hall on your left hand and go straight on and bear to the right of a group of farm buildings, through a wicket gate, and by footpath leading over to Shitlington Crags, through another wicket gate in a wall and to the top of Ealingham Rigg.

Bellingham

Bellingham lies down below by the banks of the North Tyne, and the route leads down from Ealingham Rigg to the road B6320 via

The Warks Burn

Fell End, giving a mile of road walking into the township. It seems that the old footpath leading in a direct line to the Army School Camps at Brown Rigg has fallen into disuse, but as there is a new footbridge over the Eals Burn this alternative would save some time at the end of the day.

A picturesque stone bridge built in 1835 crosses the Tyne and we enter Bellingham, 6 miles/9.6 km from Ladyhill and 207 miles/333 km from Edale. Bellingham is a plain little market town in beautiful surroundings. The architecture is dull and uninviting, perhaps still in the tradition of the turbulent old times, when the less attractive a town was the fewer temptations it offered to the lawless inhabitants of the Borderland.

Being in the direct route of the moss-troopers of Tynedale, Redesdale and Liddesdale, when riding south on their too frequent forays, it is not to be wondered that there are no traces of medieval grace or Jacobean elegance in this ancient town. From some valuable old records it appears that the name was formerly written Bellinjham, thus confirming the local pronunciation, Bellinjum.

There are some splendid old houses not far from the river, and we pass one of them, Lee Hall, on our way into the town. The house is a delightful early eighteenth century building mentioned as the probable scene of the tragical incident narrated by the Ettrick Shepherd in his *Tale of the Long Pack*, more of which will be related later. Here also was a healing spring where the lady of the hall used to dip rickety children before sunrise. After sunset on the same day they were again dipped, but in the Tyne, and their clothes were thrown into the water; if the clothes floated, so the story runs, the owner's rickets disappeared.

Half hidden among the houses is St Cuthbert's, a church of considerable interest, built about the year 1200. The church has a massive stone roof, consisting of hexagonal ribs about 3 ft/0.9 m apart, overlaid with heavy grey stone slabs. Only one other church in England (that at Barton in Cumbria) has a complete stone roof integral with the rest of the building: at Bellingham the ribs of the ceiling vault actually merge into the walls.

The necessity of such a ponderous structure will be evident when it is remembered that, according to tradition, the chancel (which

Ladyhill

Linacres

Ash

Shittington Hall

Retrospect from Eslington Rigg

Hareshaw House

Hareshaw Dene

Callerhues Crag

Blakelaw

Brown Rigg Camps

Bellingham from Ealingham Rigg

The Long Pack, St Cuthbert's churchyard, Bellingham

has had a wooden roof) was twice burnt by the Scots during the Border wars. Another illustration of the unsettled condition of the country in olden times is seen in the extremely narrow windows of the nave, widely splayed inside, which could be made available for defence purposes. The thick nave walls were heavily buttressed in the eighteenth century when they were beginning to lean outwards owing to the thrust of the roof.

The Charltons of Redesmouth, most famous of the moss-trooper families, have left their mark on local lore and legend that will not easily be forgotten. It was William Charlton of the Bower, generally spoken of as 'Bowrie', who, in 1711, encountered his arch-enemy Henry Widdrington of Buteland, in what turned out to be the last of the sword-fights that took place in the old town. Widdrington was slain in the conflict, and it was ordered that his body should be buried inside the church before Charlton's pew door, on which account, it is said, Bowrie could never again enter Bellingham church.

Episodes of this kind may have little historical importance, but they do reflect the prevailing tense atmosphere of life in North Tynedale long after the old Border forays were already matters of history, so beloved of the poets and ballad-makers.

Bellingham is the last available suitable place for supplies and accommodation, there being few habitations over the next 40 miles/ 64 km or so. Bellingham youth hostel lies on the outskirts of this ancient border town, and bed and breakfast accommodation is available at the local hotels.

The youth hostel was designed by the late John Dower, and is built in the Norwegian log-cabin style. No meals are provided and there is no store for self-cookers; the general catering position is bad, but there is a snack bar in the town where all meals may be obtained.

Notices in the youth hostel warn of the artillery ranges in Redesdale, but the Pennine Way route follows the boundary of this area for only a short distance. Otterburn Camp should be contacted beforehand, however, if it is intended for some reason to cross the ranges.

It is 15 miles/24 km from Bellingham youth hostel to the youth hostel at Byrness. This later hostel has a small store but does not provide meals, so stock up before you leave Bellingham.

The Tale of the Long Pack

Outside the churchyard are several incised sculptured grave-covers. There is also a mysterious gravestone shaped like a pedlar's pack, with carvings on it as if to represent cords, and engravings of pistols, cutlass and a whistle. Though probably medieval it has been said to be the tomb of the robber who figures in the Ettrick Shepherd's *Tale of the Long Pack*.

The story runs that in 1723 a Colonel Ridley from India retired to Lee Hall, having acquired a fortune. One winter afternoon while the family was in London a pedlar called at the house and begged a night's lodging. The sole maidservant in charge admitted him, but refused to let him stay; but she did allow him to leave a long and mysterious pack which he said he could carry no farther.

When he had gone the maidservant examined it, and to her horror thought she saw it move. She rushed out for an old farmhand and he tried to reassure her. Just then the young ploughboy entered, and hearing what had happened, fired at the pack with the gun he used for scaring crows. At once the pack heaved horribly, a great groan came from it, and a wide pool of blood gradually spread over the floor. The ploughboy had killed a robber, and on examination he was found to be armed with four loaded pistols and a cutlass.

The scared servants soon realised that this had been part of a plan for a raid on the house. They hastily set about getting help, and by nightfall twenty-five armed men were on guard. Nothing happened until one o'clock in the morning when the ploughboy sounded a silver horn he had found on the body. At once it was answered, and soon the sound of galloping hooves was heard.

As the horsemen entered the courtyard they were met with a volley from the defenders, and they fled, leaving several dead and dying men on the ground. The defenders, fearful of reprisal, dared not venture out; and when day broke it was seen that all the bodies had vanished. Significantly, members of several respectable local families were never seen again in their homes; no-one identified the man in the long-pack, and he was buried in this tomb. So the legend tells.

Bellingham to Redesdale

The Pennine Way from Bellingham now passes beyond the youth hostel on a track via Blakelaw and past Hareshaw House. Do not use the previously defined route to Hareshaw House via Hareshaw Linn, but if you wish to visit this local beauty spot do so by the proper path and retrace your steps to the village. The approach to the Linn is a most delightful walk. Just above the railway the path crosses heaps of shale left behind by the deserted ironworks and skirts a long-neglected dam before the romantic glen reveals itself. The steep and rocky sides of the dene are covered with birches, rowans and ferns, and the rough and narrow pathway leads up and down amongst the trees, crossing and recrossing the stream by wooden bridges.

The lower fall is first reached, a perpendicular ledge of rock 20 ft/6 m high, over which the stream falls in a twin cascade. Half a mile/0.8 km further the main fall of Hareshaw Linn is reached, a shimmering veil of water tumbling over a 60 ft/18 m high ledge which completely seals off the head of the dene, and falling into a gloomy chasm.

> With a sudden dash and a bound and splash,
> With a rout and shout and roar and din,
> The brook, amaz'd, alarm'd and craz'd,
> Is sprawling into Hareshaw Linn.
> 'Tween wooded cliffs, fern-fringed, in falls,
> All broken into spray and foam.

> J. Clephan

Beyond Hareshaw House the Pennine Way passes west of Abbey Rigg and to the Otterburn road near an old coal mine. Cross the road B6320 and make a line due north to Lough Shaw, 1,102 ft/ 336 m, and Deer Play, 1,183 ft/361 m. Then cross north-westerly along the line of a parish boundary, passing over Lord's Shaw, 1,167 ft/356 m to a road.

We have now come 7 miles/11.2 km from Bellingham, and from

The Linn at the head of Hareshaw Dene

Lough Shaw from the B.6320 north of Bellingham

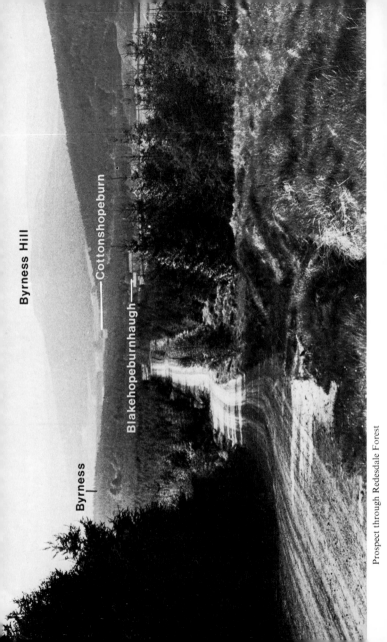

Byrness Hill

Byrness

Cottonshopeburn

Blakehopeburnhaugh

Prospect through Redesdale Forest

The church and hotel at Byrness

this point the official route follows a line leading across open country and giving unrivalled views of the Rede valley and the Border and Cheviot hills. The old route past Pit Houses and Gib Shiel is open to motor vehicles and has been relegated in favour of the open moor, but is an alternative in bad weather.

From the road continue north-westerly, keeping a wire fence on your right, past the monument on Padon Hill, 1,240 ft/378 m, and down to a stone wall in the Gib Shiel valley. Turn right through a wicket gate, around the wall corner, back through another wicket gate and continue uphill keeping the stone wall on your right to Brownrigg Head, 1,191 ft/363 m. Turn northwest keeping a wire fence on your right and follow it for a mile/1.6 km to the corner of Redesdale Forest. Cross the fence and continue in the same north-west direction between it and the trees for another ¼-mile/0.4 km to Rookengate, where the road from Gib Shiel enters the forest at height 1,140 ft/347 m.

Redesdale Forest

From the gate the track drops steadily through the forest, and splendid panoramic views open out, extending from Rochester over the northern Cheviots to the Border crossing at Carter Bar. Within 4 miles/6.4 km the track leads to Blakehopeburnhaugh (pronounced 'Blakeupburnhaf') and after crossing a Bailey bridge bears right and crosses a second bridge over the River Rede, and leads to the main Newcastle–Jedburgh road, route A68, ½-mile/0.8 km distant.

Just short of the main road there is a turn left along the line of overhead power cables through fields to Cottonshopeburn Foot. A track crosses to the left of the farm buildings and over the Rede, and we follow this for ½-mile/0.8 km to Raw. A footbridge takes us over the Rede yet again, and the track continues through the Forestry Commission's 'The Raw' picnic area to emerge at the main road by a little stone-tiled church and opposite the Byrness Hotel, a distance of 223 miles/358 km from Edale.

Byrness

Byrness is one of six villages in the Border Forest Park specially built to house forestry workers. All designed by Thomas Sharp, the

National Park Information Centre and Youth Hostel, Byrness

internationally famous rural and town planner, Byrness was built in 1951. Not all the houses are occupied now: one is an information centre for the Northumberland National Park, and adjoining it are two others which have been converted into a youth hostel. (The hostel is reached by taking the forestry track parallel to A68 running westwards from the church.) Other accommodation in Redesdale is scarce. The Byrness Hotel makes ramblers welcome with hot baths and good meals, and the petrol filling station opposite has a cafeteria.

The tiny village church of old Byrness contains a remarkable window 'in memory of those men, women and children who have died during the construction of the reservoir at Catcleugh'. The glass shows workmen labouring with barrow, pick and shovel on the construction of the reservoir, with an engine and trucks beside them; and a child sitting on the ground with her father's dinner in a handkerchief. Above is a medallion portraying a saw, an axe, and a maul. A thousand men took fifteen years to build this huge reservoir. It has a capacity of 2,305 million gallons/10 478 million litres and supplies Newcastle, 40 miles/64 km away, with 10 million gallons/45 million litres of water daily.

The last stretch of our journey along the Pennine Way involves 27 miles/43 km of very tough going along the highest ridge of the Cheviots. Almost trackless peat hag and bog, the route must be covered in one day, unless you expect to use the occasional farms in Upper Coquetdale for overnight accommodation. However, magnificent views far into Scotland compensate for the rough going. Dere Street, The Street and Clennell Street provide convenient escape routes from the ridge if the weather turns bad on your day's march. There are two bad-weather shelters on the Pennine Way in the Cheviots: one at 1,472 ft/448 m on Yearning Saddle, SW of Lamb Hill at NGR 805129, and one at 1,631 ft/497 m above Hen Hole at 877202. Neither are to be relied upon as overnight shelter in winter except in an emergency—i.e. don't plan beforehand to sleep out in them, but use them if caught out in bad weather and if you cannot reach the escape routes.

Redesdale to Lamb Hill

The great green bastions of the Cheviot Hills (pronounced
'Cheeveot') form some of the finest scenery in Northumberland.
They also form a natural barrier between England and Scotland, as
they extend for about 35 miles/56 km and cover some 200 sq
miles/518 sq kms of Northumberland and another 100 sq miles/259
sq kms of Roxburghshire.

The steep slopes and uplands of these hills are tenanted by hardy
flocks of Cheviot sheep, which retain much of their wild nature. The
Cheviots are important sheep country, and two main breeds are to
be seen on these hills. The Cheviot breed is kept on the lower land,
while the Blackface roam the bleaker heights. The Cheviot is short-
wooled, white-faced and hornless, but is best distinguished with its
Elizabethan ruff: the Blackface is a horned species with a Roman
nose. A more hardy strain than the pure breeds is produced by
cross-breeding Cheviot rams with Blackface ewes. The shepherds
who live lonely lives in these hills spin their own wool in the winter,
and in the summer tend flocks sent from other districts.

Like most hills, the Cheviots have a character all of their own,
and to appreciate them it is best to follow the advice of the poet
Thomas Pringle, and

> Let our pilgrim footsteps seek
> Old Cheviot's pathless mossy peak;
> For there the Mountain Spirit still
> Lingers round the mountain hill.

Byrness to Chew Green
From the Byrness Hotel to Chew Green is a hill walk of 5 miles/8
km. The route takes a forest ride about 200 yds/182 m west of the
hotel. Pass some cottages, go through a gate and turn sharp right
then left straight up the hillside to the ruins of the fire look-out post
on Byrness Hill, 1,358 ft/414 m. This gives a grand view over
Redesdale and the Catcleugh Reservoir, with the new Byrness
village far away below.

Byrness Hill

Windy Crag

Forest Ride

Hotel

Byrness in Redesdale

Windy Crag   Houx Hill   Saughy Crag   Byrness Hill

Byrness and the Cheviots

The border fence at Coquet Head

Proceeding due north over the open fell it is a simple matter to follow the watershed, which leads over Houx Hill, Windy Crag and Ravens Knowe to Ogre Hill, where a track descends to the Border and Coquet Head.

You now stand at the headwaters of three rivers: southward run tributaries of the Rede towards the Tyne; to the west and north a group of burns wind through Leithope Forest to form the Kale Water which feeds the Tweed; to the east the Coquet begins its meandering course through the Cheviots towards Rothbury. The Tweed basin stretches out to the north-west, while to the north-east the trackless green hills heave like waves of the sea towards the great square mass of the Cheviot, 12 miles/19 km distant.

The Border here runs down the course of the Coquet and soon reaches the bold rectangular outlines of the great Roman camps of Chew Green. This route runs just inside the safety zone to the west of a firing range, and is marked with Ministry of Defence posts. This area is not used much, but during the summer months it is unsafe to attempt any return that leads farther EAST.

Redesdale Artillery Range is a vast military training ground, which began as a comparatively circumscribed area near Rochester in Redesdale, but enlarged during the Second World War to take in an enormous tract of country, some 70 sq mls/181 sq kms in extent. The range is officially closed to the public when firing is in progress, and this is indicated by the flying of red flags.

Chew Green Roman Camps
Chew Green Camps are sited on a small triangular plateau which formed for the Romans the only suitable camping ground in most difficult country. The camps lie beside the old Roman road of Dere Street which formed the main road into Scotland from the northern military headquarters of York, and are known to have been in use between AD 78 and 185. Temporary camps and permanent forts were crowded into this restricted space until the site became the most complicated and remarkable group of earthworks in the Roman Empire. As the earthworks overlap they are not easy to understand, but they are plainly visible on the bare hillside from the vantage point of Harden Edge.

The Roman Camps of Chew Green from Harden Edge

Brownhart Law

Dere Street

The biggest is the Great South Camp, covering 22 acres/8.9 ha of the best and driest ground. The Great North Camp covers 15 acres/6 ha, but the best preserved is the West Camp of 6¼ acres/2.5 ha, with notably high and clearly marked ramparts. The South East Fort, about 2 acres/0.8 ha, also has a bold rampart and ditch, while the East Fort has the foundations of a medieval chapel in the middle.

The site must have been an obvious choice as the halting place of the Roman armies marching to the north and as permanent quarters for patrol garrisons, but surrounded by dark hills and monotonous moorland the position of the legionaries in this station must have been one of considerable hardship and discomfort.

The Border: Chew Green to Windy Gyle 6 miles/9.6 km
Dere Street was built by Agricola from York to Scotland, and approaching Chew Green the road becomes known as Gammel's Path, probably from the Danish 'gamel,' meaning old. This was an appointed meeting place of the English and Scottish Lord's Wardens of the Marches for punishing offenders against the Border Laws and settling disputes by single combat; the men of Coquetdale and Redesdale were frequently here for this purpose, and the road was also much used by drovers and smugglers of salt and whisky.

Dere Street and the Pennine Way cross the Coquet stream and turn sharply northwards to run round the shoulder of Brownhart Law, 1,664 ft/507 m, to the Border. On the summit of Brownhart Law, a few yards beyond a wicket gate, is a Roman long-distance signalling-post, from which there is a view of the hills of seven counties.

Twenty-four cairns built with peat sods and topped with temporary notice boards have been erected marking the route of the Pennine Way on the Border; twelve between Brownhart Law and Mozie Law and another twelve between Butt Roads and the Cheviot. Although the Border fence is nonexistent in most parts, the summit ridge is easy to follow except in most severe weather, and then care must be exercised in case the wrong fence is followed, especially in the vicinity of Lamb Hill, Score Head and on Cheviot. Two refuges have been erected for bad weather shelter at 805129 and 877202.

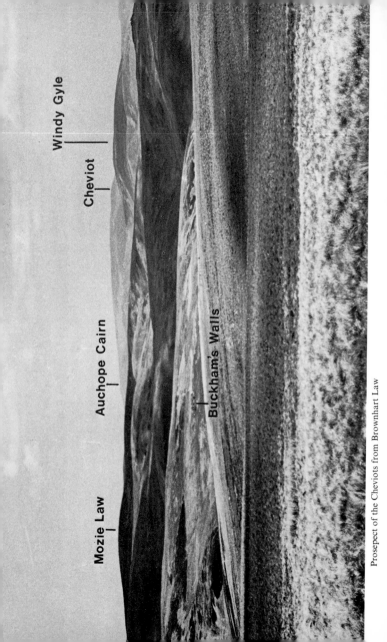

Prospect of the Cheviots from Brownhart Law

From Brownhart Law the route leads northwards to Black Halls and height 1,464 ft/461 m, then contours round between Broad Flow and Wedder Hill, round the head of Rennies Burn, resuming the Border fence at Lamb Hill, 1,677 ft/511 m. Just before this is reached, at NGR 805129, is the first of two bad weather refuges. Then follows Beefstand Hill, 1,842 ft/561 m, and Mozie Law, 1,812 ft/552 m.

Between Mozie Law and Windy Rigg 'The Street' crosses the watershed from the Kale Water to Upper Coquetdale. From 'The Street' crossing, the Pennine Way leads eastwards over Windy Rigg to Windy Gyle, 2,036 ft/619 m, 8 miles/12.8 km from Chew Green, 13 miles/21 km from Byrness and 14 miles/22.5 km from our destination in Kirk Yetholm. Russell's Cairn is a huge stone tumulus on the summit, said to be the burial place of Sir Francis Russell, who lost his life at Hexpethgate in July 1585 in one of those unfortunate affrays into which the meetings of the Lord's Wardens of the Marches all too frequently developed.

Windy Gyle affords a splendid view of the English side of the hills, while the whole of the Border ridge is in view to the 'stone men' on Auchope Cairn. Half a mile/0.8 km north-east of Windy Gyle we come to another cairn, formerly named Russell's Cairn. Both cairns are probably Bronze Age burial mounds, for the Cheviots are rich in ancient earthworks, hill-forts and homesteads.

Windy Gyle to Cheviot 5 miles/8 km

A mile and a half/2.4 km beyond Windy Gyle a gate in the Border fence marks the crossing of Clennell Street, a grass-grown track crossing the watershed. Clennell Street is not a Roman road, as its name might be thought to imply, but a prehistoric trackway. In the Middle Ages it was known as Hexpethgate at the Border crossing, and it is now usually called Cocklawgate. Cock Law, the protruding ridge on the Scottish side, was one of the recognised places for the meetings of the Lord's Wardens of the Marches.

In adverse weather conditions it is best to avoid Cheviot, so descend Clennell Street on the Scottish side to Bowmont Water— the easy and safe way out of troubles—but after Bowmont Water there is a 7 mile/11.2 km road walk into Kirk Yetholm.

Lamb Hill to Kirk Yetholm

Auchope Cairn

Cheviot

Comb Fell

The Cheviot from Russell's Cairn on Windy Gyle

If accommodation is required, the isolated farm at Uswayford, 1.5 mls/2.4 km off the Pennine Way, down Clennell Street on the English side, can provide bed and breakfast and evening meals.

It has been an easy walk down from Windy Gyle, but to follow the Border towards Cheviot is a much lengthier and laborious process. Continue on to Butt Roads, 1,718 ft/524 m, King's Seat, 1,743 ft/531 m, Score Head, 1,910 ft/582 m, and Cairn Hill, 2,545 ft/776 m, where the Pennine Way thrusts out a spur to the summit of Cheviot, 2,676 ft/815 m, 5 miles/8 km from Windy Gyle.

The Cheviot

Cheviot can be seen from so many places that it might be thought to afford wide views, but this is by no means the case. Daniel Defoe, during his grand tour of Scotland in 1726, was prompted by 'curiosity of no extraordinary kind' to make an expedition to the summit of what was then practically an unknown hill. Defoe feared that there might not be room for all of his party to stand on the top, but there is in fact a flat summit of some 50 acres/20 ha, and views can be enjoyed only by walking round the edge of it. To make matters worse the plateau is covered by an extensive waste of peat hags and bog, so that steady progress over it is at any time difficult and after heavy rain is not worth attempting.

Snow generally lies upon Cheviot during half the year, and in severe winters has been known to remain in the highest ravines from September to July. Strewn on the heather, bracken and grass slopes lie grey rocks of porphyry, syentie, dolerite and pink granite. Among the coarse wiry grass and bog-mosses grow several mountain plants—the cloudberry or mountain bramble, whose scarlet berries, becoming yellow when they ripen, are scattered over the waste like gems; the red whortle-berry or cowberry; the crowberry, the bilberry, cotton grass, cow wheat, rigid carex and three species of clubmoss.

A heap of stones called the Western Cairn is the highest point, and not far away is a deep crater filled to the rim with water. This marks the scene of a tragedy, when in December, 1944, a Flying Fortress of the USAAF laden with bombs on its way to Germany, crashed during a late afternoon blizzard. The two shepherds who saved the seven crew—two were killed in the crash—received the British Empire Medal; and their sheepdog that found them became the first animal, other than one actually serving with the armed or civil defence forces, to receive the Dickin Medal—the animals' Victoria Cross.

The view from the plateau ridge is most extensive—north to the Lammermuir Hills of Scotland beyond the Tweed, west to the 'three peaked Eildons', south to the uplands of Durham, and east to the coast and the Farne Islands, Holy Island and Coquet Island standing out from the blue, green and grey waters. South-west is the prospect of the long line of the conical, grass-covered summits of the Cheviot range.

Cheviot to Auchope Cairn 2 miles/3.2 km

From Cheviot summit return to Cairn Hill and the Border fence, at a height of 2,300 ft/701 m passing the Hanging Stone, a rock which derives its name from the circumstance of a packman being strangled by his pack slipping over the edge and tightening the strap around his neck. This fractured rocky outcrop, 17 ft/5 m high, is now 200 yds/182 m inside England, though in medieval times was actually on the Border, and in addition formed the boundary of the Eastern and Middle Marches.

Half a mile/0.8 km north-west is Auchope Cairn, 2,382 ft/726 m, a prominent peak on the Border, distinguished by several large cairns on the crest of its narrow ridge. It has one of the widest views in Britain, and with binoculars it is possible to see the mountain Lochnagar by Balmoral, well over 100 miles/160 km away in the Highlands.

The Hen Hole

To the north of Auchope Cairn is the chasm of Hen Hole, so deep and so narrow that the sun never enters it, and often holding a small patch of snow even at midsummer. Black cliffs rise steeply to a height of 250 ft/76 m on either side of this lonely and lovely ravine, where raven and peregrine falcon nest on inaccessible ledges. From the summit of Cheviot a peaty burn splashes down from ledge to ledge forming pretty waterfalls, fringed with ferns and mosses, and

Auchope Cairn from height 2,419 ft near Cairn Hill

The Schil ▸

Hen Hole

Prospect into Scotland from Auchope Cairn

The Village Green at Kirk Yetholm, and the end of the Pennine Way issuing from the dreadful gorge of the College Burn.

The Hen Hole is a famous hunting ground for the botanist, who will find in its rock recesses or the vicinity the star saxifrage, the cut-leaved or mossy saxifrage, alpine sowthistle, chickweed epilobe, the rare dwarf cornel, green spleenwort, teeth fern, curled or parsley fern, floating sweet grass or Balfour's pea, serrated winter green and black willow.

Foxes are occasionally hunted into the Hole, and there is a tradition of a party of huntsmen being lured into the chasm by the sweetest music they had ever heard, and could never again find their way out. Apart from being the haunt of fairies, local legend asserts that this gloomy gorge was the hiding place of Black Adam of Cheviot, one of the most notorious of Borderland freebooters, who murdered the bride of Wight Fletcher at Wooperton. Scott, in his *Minstrelsy of the Scottish Border*, tells the ballad of Black Adam bursting in upon a wedding party when the bridegroom was away to fetch the priest, robbing the women guests of their jewels and ravishing and killing the bride. On his return Fletcher tracked the murderer to the Hen Hole, but Black Adam escaped the bridegroom by a desperate leap of seven yards or more into his lair, a cave in the side of the steep cliff.

Descent to Kirk Yetholm

From Auchope Cairn the Border fence is followed westerly over Auchope Rigg, past the second bad-weather refuge at NGR 877202 (1631 ft/497 m), then northerly to the Schil, 1,985 ft/605 m, a prominent cone with distinctive rocks around its summit, possibly a Bronze Age burial cairn.

On the descent towards Kirk Yetholm the Pennine Way now takes a new line on an official route approved by the Countryside Commission for Scotland. In order to avoid the metalled road down the Halterburn valley, the Pennine Way Council suggested an alternative and this has been way-marked by Borders Regional Council.

Descend from the Schil NW: cross the stone wall by a ladder stile into Scotland, and follow the track to the col between Black Hag and the Curr. A cairn with a signpost and an inset map mark the point where the old Pennine Way descended to Burnhead: we now keep to the R. meet the Border, following it due N on its gradual descent of Steer Rig and over the broad back of White Law. Descend White Law NW to Whitelaw Nick, cross the Border, due N on a well-defined track, a lovely old grass track going north-west below the Iron Age fort on Green Humbleton Hill and down to the metalled road in the Halterburn valley. It is but a short mile along the road to Kirk Yetholm and the end of the Pennine Way.

Kirk Yetholm is a place of some antiquity, and was once the 'capital' of the notorious gipsy clan of the Faas that once flourished in the Border. A row of houses across the green from the pleasant Border Hotel is still called Gipsy Row, and a small cottage above this with an ivy-fronted porch was known as the Gipsy Palace. Kirk Yetholm had an evil reputation in those days, but the 'dynasty' declined, and the last 'queen', Esther Fall (or Faa) Blyth, was buried in the churchyard in 1835.

It has been a long stretch of 27 miles/43 km without shelter from Byrness, but Kirk Yetholm can provide accommodation at the Hartleyburn Private Hotel or the Scottish Youth Hostel. The hostel is well equipped for self cookers though no meals are provided, and enquiries from the warden will direct you to a cottage where good meals will be provided, including an early breakfast so as to enable you to catch the early bus to Kelso. Kelso is the nearest town of any size with public transport to take you back home in comfort.

On the Pennine Way you have enjoyed magnificent scenery, with wooded valleys, barren moorlands, tumbling waterfalls, Roman roads and old bridleways, wild life but above all the get-away-from-it-all feeling that only the hills can give. If you were not fit at the start you should be now, and if you have walked the whole Way you will have the satisfaction of having completed the most demanding long-distance footpath in Britain. Congratulations!

Weary with toil, I haste me to my bed,
The dear repose for limbs with travel tir'd;
But then begins a journey in my head,
To work my mind, when body's work's expir'd.

William Shakespeare

Title	*Author*	*Publisher*
The Pennine Way	K. Oldham	Dalesman 1960
Walking the Pennine Way	A. P. Binns	Gerrard 1966
The Pennine Way in 20 days	H. O. Wade	Harold Hill 1966
The Shell Book of the Pennine Way	M. Marriott	Queen Anne press 1968
Pennine Way Companion	A. Wainwright	Westmorland Gazette 1968
The Pennine Way	T. Stephenson	HMSO 1969
Along the Pennine Way	J. H. B. Peel	Cassell 1969
A Walker on The Pennine Way	C. Walker	Pendyke Publications 1974
Mountain Trail	J. Wood	Allen & Unwin 1947
North to South along the Pennine Way	G. Hardy	Frederick Warne 1985
Wainright on the Pennine Way	A. Wainright	Michael Joseph 1985
One Man and his Bog	B. Pilton	Corgi 1986
Going Dutch (on) The Pennine Way	G. C. de Waal	Gédéwé (Holland) 1987
Day by day along The Pennine Way	J. J. Fleming	Trelawney Press (Morecambe) 1986
Pennine Way North National Trail Guide	T. Hopkins	Arum Press/ Countryside Commission Ordnance Survey 1989
Peak Panorama	W. A. Poucher	Chapman & Hall 1946
Backbone of England	W. A. Poucher	Country Life 1946
Peak & Pennines	W. A. Poucher	Constable 1966
High Peak	E. Byne & G. J. Sutton	Secker & Warburgh 1966
Buildings of England	N. Pevsner	Penguin 1959
Scenery of England & Wales	A. E. Trueman	Gollancz 1938
Wild Flowers of Chalk & Limestone	J. F. Lousley	Collins 1950
Wanderings in the Pennines	W. T. Palmer	Skeffington 1951
The Kings England Series	A. Mee	Hodder & Stoughton 1936–52
Peak District National Park		HMSO 1960
The Peak District	K. C. Edwards	Collins 1962

Lancashire & the Pennines	F. Singleton	Batsford 1952
The Roof of Lancashire	H. C. Collins	Dent 1950
Striding Through Yorkshire	A. J. Brown	Country Life 1949
Yorkshire & the North East	A. Raistrick	Oliver & Boyd 1963
Comprehensive Guide to Northumberland	W. W. Tomlinson	W. Scott 1935
Border National Forest Park		HMSO 1958
Guide to the Cheviot Hills	F. R. Banks	Reid 1950
Scottish Border Country	F. R. Banks	Batsford 1951
Handbook of the Roman Wall	C. Bruce	Reid 1957

Index